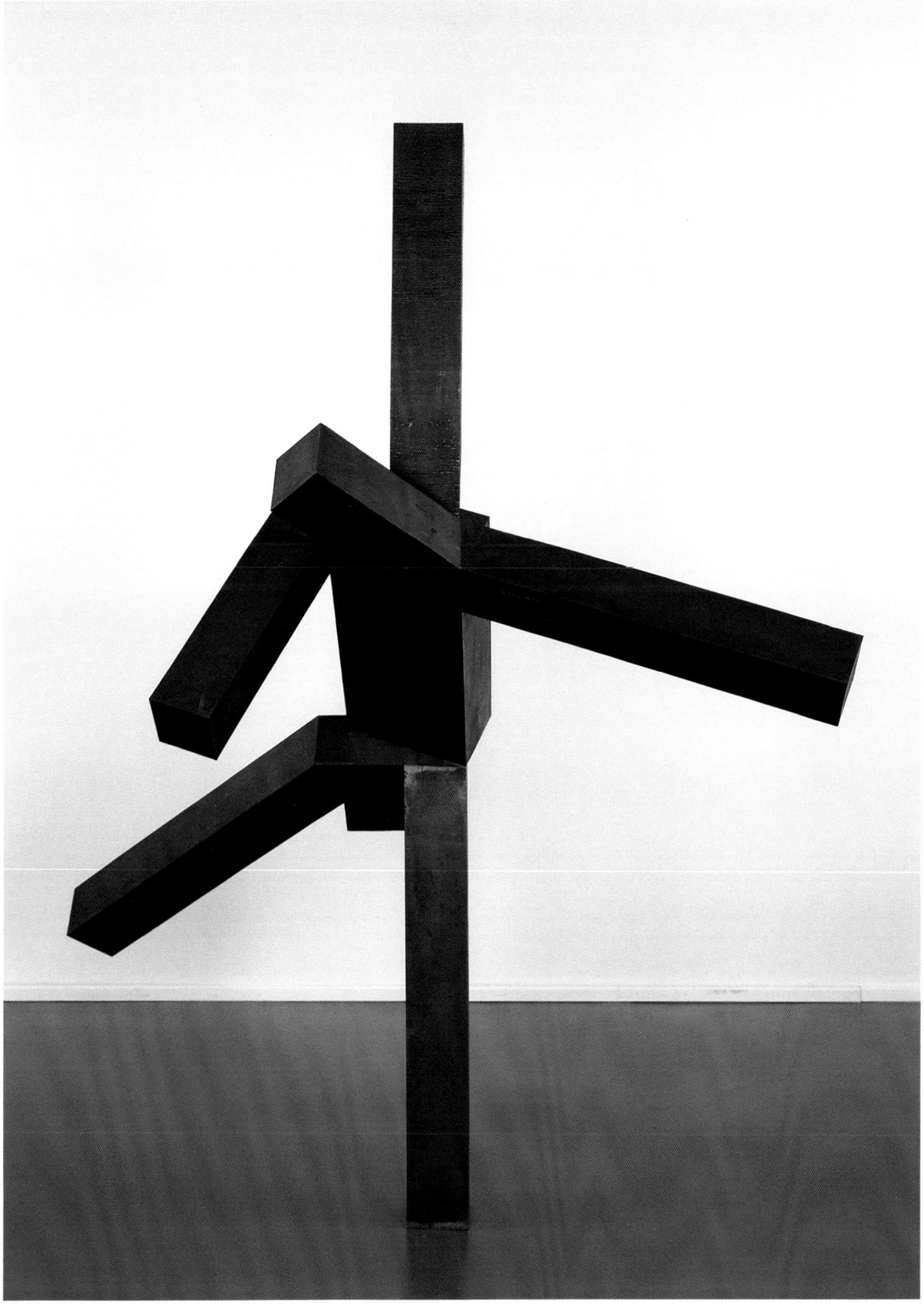

Fig. 1   Untitled, 1982
bronze   2/3
73 x 70 x 30″
Collection of the Museum of Contemporary Art,
Los Angeles
The Barry Lowen Collection

The John and Mable Ringling Museum of Art
Sarasota, Florida

October 31 - December 14, 1986

© Copyright 1986 by
The John and Mable Ringling Museum of Art Foundation
5401 Bayshore Road
Sarasota, Florida 34243

All rights reserved
Library of Congress Card No. 86-82010
ISBN No. 0-916758-22-2
Design: The Graphics Design Center
Photography:
    Howard Agriesti: p. 11.
    Geoffrey Clements: p. 5, 12, 13, 15, 16, 19, 22, 24, 25, 26,
                27, 29, 30, 31, 34.
    D. James Dee: p. 3, 4, 6, 10, 14, 17, 21, 28.
    Judy Linn: p. 32.
    Museum of Fine Arts, Boston: p. 20.
    Squidds & Nunns: foreword.
Printing: Coastal Printing Inc.

Joel Shapiro

Joel Shapiro

Joel Shapiro

Sculpture and Drawings 1981-85

Mark Ormond

THE JOHN AND MABLE RINGLING MUSEUM OF ART
OCTOBER 31 - DECEMBER 14, 1986

LENDERS TO THE EXHIBITION

Mr. & Mrs. Robert Buford
Paula Cooper Gallery, New York
Dallas Museum of Art
The Detroit Institute of Arts
Mr. & Mrs. Gilbert Edelson
The Collection of Exxon Corporation
General Mills Art Collection
Keny and Johnson Gallery
The Museum of Contemporary Art, Los Angeles,
The Barry Lowen Collection
Museum of Fine Arts, Boston
The Newark Museum
Private Collection, Boston
Mr. & Mrs. Robert Quinn
Joel Shapiro
Mr. & Mrs. A. Skeppner

TABLE OF CONTENTS

PREFACE

This October the Museum will present a major exhibition of the sculpture and drawings of Joel Shapiro. The exhibition, organized by the Museum's Curator of Exhibitions and one of its experts in the area of modern art, Mark Ormond, is elegant, sophisticated, and challenging. The Museum is proud to present this important work to the Florida public.

Last October the Museum presented a major exhibition of the work of Francesco Clemente. This exhibition is still traveling to other museums in the United States and reflects the insight and critical ability of its excellent curator, Michael Auping, then a member of the Museum staff.

The Francesco Clemente and Joel Shapiro exhibitions in their quality and diversity nicely represent both the diversity and high standards of contemporary art. Both present art which by its intellectual challenge and its multi-faceted ironies reflects the difficulties that an unprepared audience might have in approaching important contemporary art of even the highest quality.

These exhibitions of The John and Mable Ringling Museum of Art also demonstrate the commitment of the Museum to contemporary art and the development and education of its audience in Florida. The Museum has now devoted two major staff positions to the area of contemporary art, has entered into a vibrant acquisition program in the area, is planning the development of permanent galleries of contemporary art, and is deepening the scope of the educational programs surrounding these activities. Contemporary art then forms a counterpoint to the Museum's well established collections in seventeenth and eighteenth-century art.

Although acknowledgements are made below, I wish to thank Mark Ormond for his marvelous work on this fine exhibition, the Board of Directors, the State of Florida, the Museum's Foundation, and all those who have made this splendid presentation of the important work of Joel Shapiro available to the people of Florida.

Laurence J. Ruggiero
Director

INTRODUCTION

After a decade of critical acclaim, Joel Shapiro's position as a major American artist was confirmed in 1982 when he was accorded a retrospective exhibition at the Whitney Museum of American Art. At that time, his sculpture was beginning to deal almost exclusively with the human figure, an orientation that had surfaced with considerable regularity in the late 1970s as he moved away from the motif of the house. The sculpture of the past four years has confirmed this preoccupation with the human form. The majority of the work can be described as anthropomorphic, for the figure can be seen hidden in the geometry of Shapiro's abstraction. Equally important, the sculpture has displayed a stylistic homogeneity that was not present in the '70s, when Shapiro often worked with several themes and motifs at the same time. The sculpture of the '80s displays a Constructivist approach of building form through the addition of distinct units. As never before, Shapiro has made one sculpture by working out of the formal implications of the preceding one. The bond is so tight that there is often a direct relationship between them, as parts of one sculpture appear in the composition of a second, very different, piece.

The work of the past four years has confirmed the observation made by Roberta Smith in her essay in the Whitney catalogue that Shapiro is an artist "just hitting his stride." The works in this exhibition, which date from 1981 to 1985, have been chosen to display this artistic growth. In addition to twelve sculptures, twelve charcoal drawings have been included. The latter are exciting works in their own right and stand as some of the finest drawings of the twentieth century. For Shapiro, unlike for most sculptors, drawing does not function as the mere handmaiden of sculpture; while it shares the same formal concerns, rarely can it be seen as a study for a specific three-dimensional work. Shapiro has a wonderful affinity for charcoal, and through manipulation of the medium he is able to endow the drawings with the same psychological and physical richness found in the sculpture.

This exhibition would not have been possible without the generous assistance of Joel Shapiro, who gave me access to his home, studio, and foundry so I could study his work, and who provided numerous opportunities for me to discuss his art with him.

I am most grateful to Paula Cooper and her staff at the Paula Cooper Gallery. Special thanks must be extended to Douglas Baxter, Director, Carol Caldwell, Steven Wolfe, and Julie Graham. Bertha Sarmina, Joel Shapiro's assistant, was invaluable for coordinating the details of the exhibition at the studio.

I would like to thank the following lenders for the generosity of sharing their sculptures and drawings: Mr. and Mrs. Robert Buford; Paula Cooper Gallery; Dallas Museum of Art; The Detroit Institute of Arts; Mr. and Mrs. Gilbert Edelson; The Collection of Exxon Corporation; General Mills Art Collection; Keny and Johnson Gallery; The Museum of Contemporary Art, Los Angeles; Museum of Fine Arts, Boston; The Newark Museum; Mr. and Mrs. Robert Quinn; Joel Shapiro; Mr. and Mrs. A. Skeppner; and a Boston private collector. For their special consideration and assistance of loan requests, I would like to thank the following individuals: Lois Dickson and her assistant Susan Jones at Exxon Corporation, Sue Graze at the Dallas Museum of Art, Melissa Hough at the CIGNA Collection, Don McNeil at the General Mills Collection, Gary Reynolds at The Newark Museum, and Barbara Stern Shapiro at the Museum of Fine Arts, Boston. I greatly appreciate the kindness of the many individuals not participating in the exhibition who allowed me access to their collections. In particular, I would like to thank Mr. and Mrs. Jay Bennett, Douglas S. Cramer and Marcia Harrow, all of whom were most supportive.

I must thank Peder Bonnier and Debbie Grant for the role they played in introducing me to Joel Shapiro and for their constant moral support. I am also extremely grateful to Jan Silberstein for the personal attention she gave to many of the details of the exhibition and the catalogue, and for her steadfast support over the years for the Ringling Museum's twentieth-century projects. My thanks to Erwin Johanningmeier for editing an early draft of the essay.

The production of the catalogue and the installation of the exhibition are the result of the efforts of many of my colleagues at the Ringling Museum. I am grateful to Elizabeth Telford and her staff for seeing to the many details of shipping and installation; Elaine Chamberlain for typing loans and the catalogue manuscript; Lynell Morr for securing important research material and for a thoughtful reading of the text; Susan Burkhart and Myriam Springuel for helpful ideas about the manuscript; Arden McKennee for proofreading; and Nancy Glaser and her staff in Education for assistance with interpretive programs. I am particularly grateful to Marianna Adams for her collaboration on the gallery guide and for her moral support at many crucial stages of this project.

My colleagues in the Curatorial Department, Cynthia Duval, Anthony Janson, and Joseph Jacobs, have been a constant source of ideas, encouragement, and support. I would particularly like to thank Joseph Jacobs for his enthusiastic support of the project and for his humor that sustained me through the seemingly endless task of preparing the final manuscript.

Most important, I would like to thank the Board of Trustees and the Director, Dr. Laurence J. Ruggiero, for their continuing support of twentieth-century art, which has made this exhibition possible.

Mark Ormond
Curator of Exhibitions

Sculpture

Sculpture

Sculpture

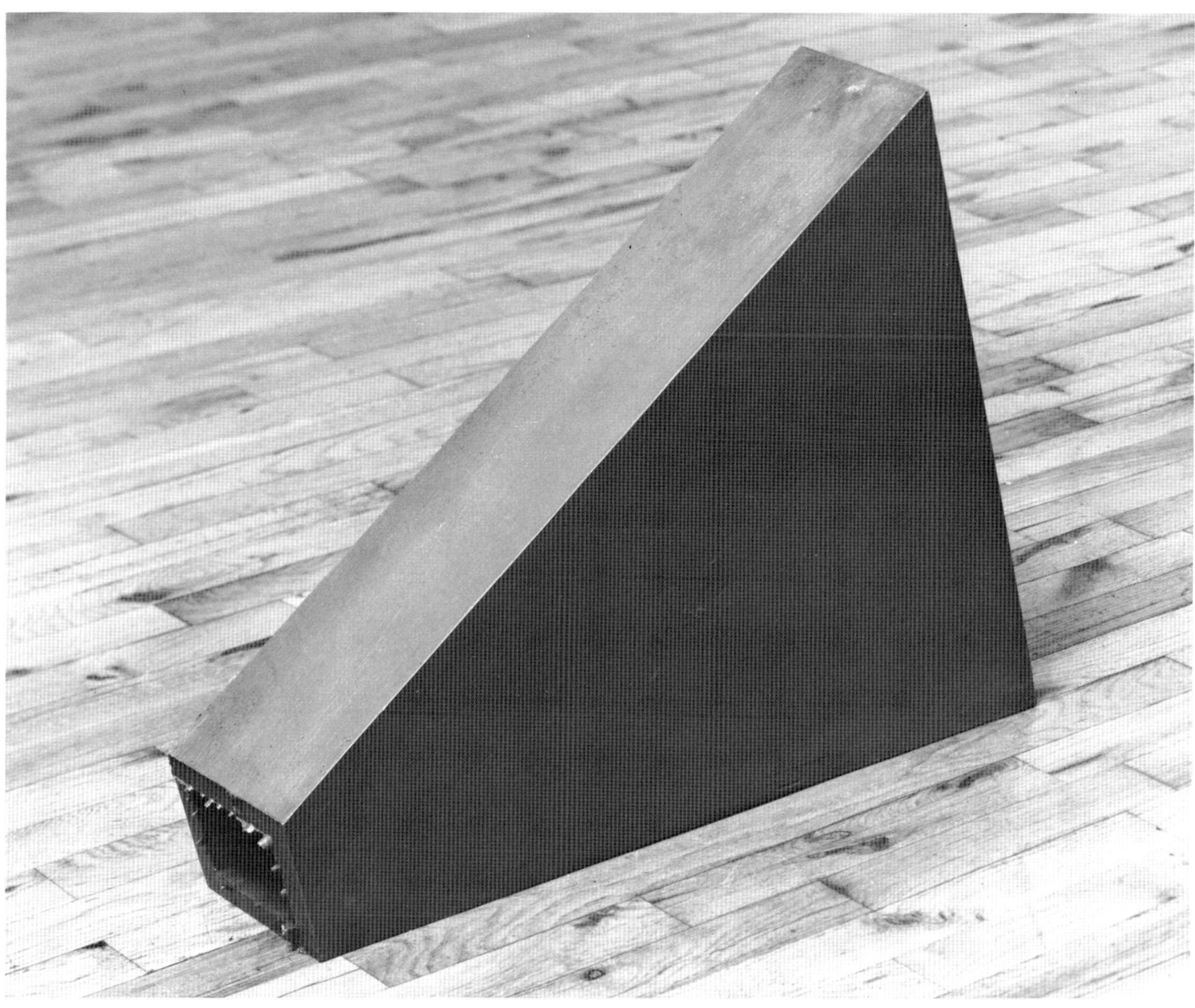

Fig. 2 Untitled, 1984
cast iron
21½ x 29¼ x 5¾"
Courtesy Paula Cooper Gallery, New York

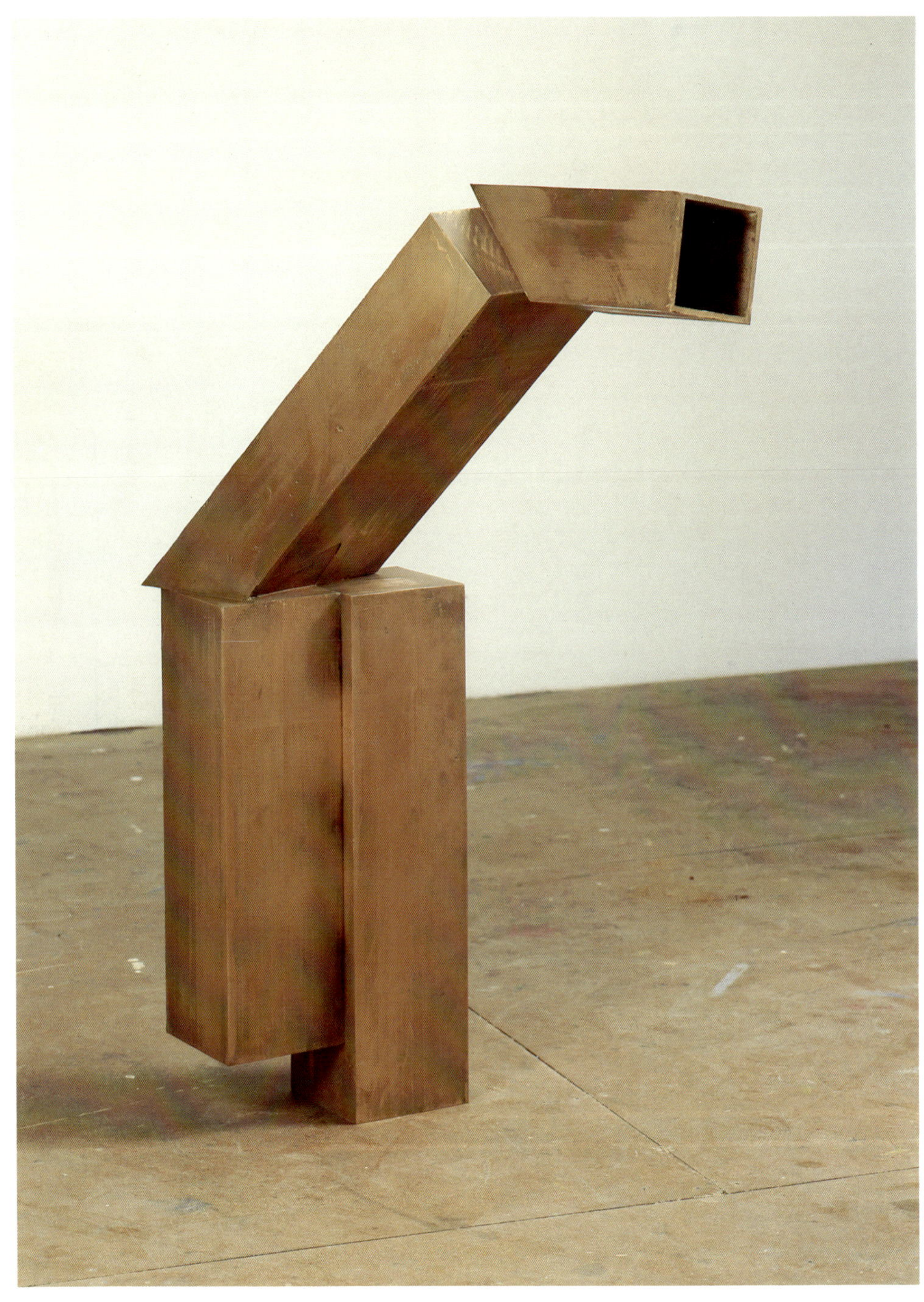

Fig. 3 Untitled, 1985
bronze   A.P.
38½ x 28½ x 14″
Collection of the Artist

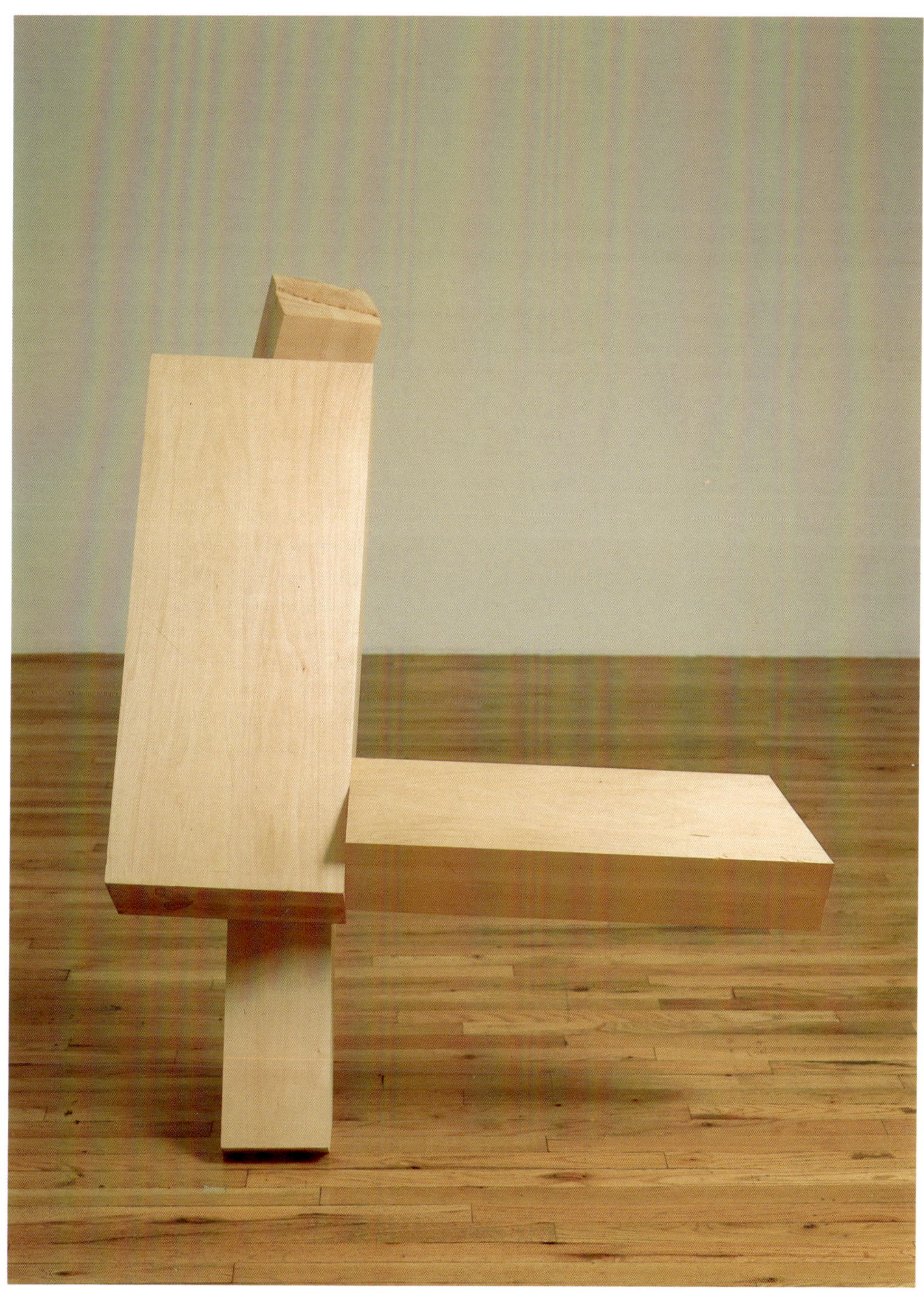

Fig. 4   Untitled, 1982-83
Bass wood
45½ x 38½ x 26½"
Collection of the Artist

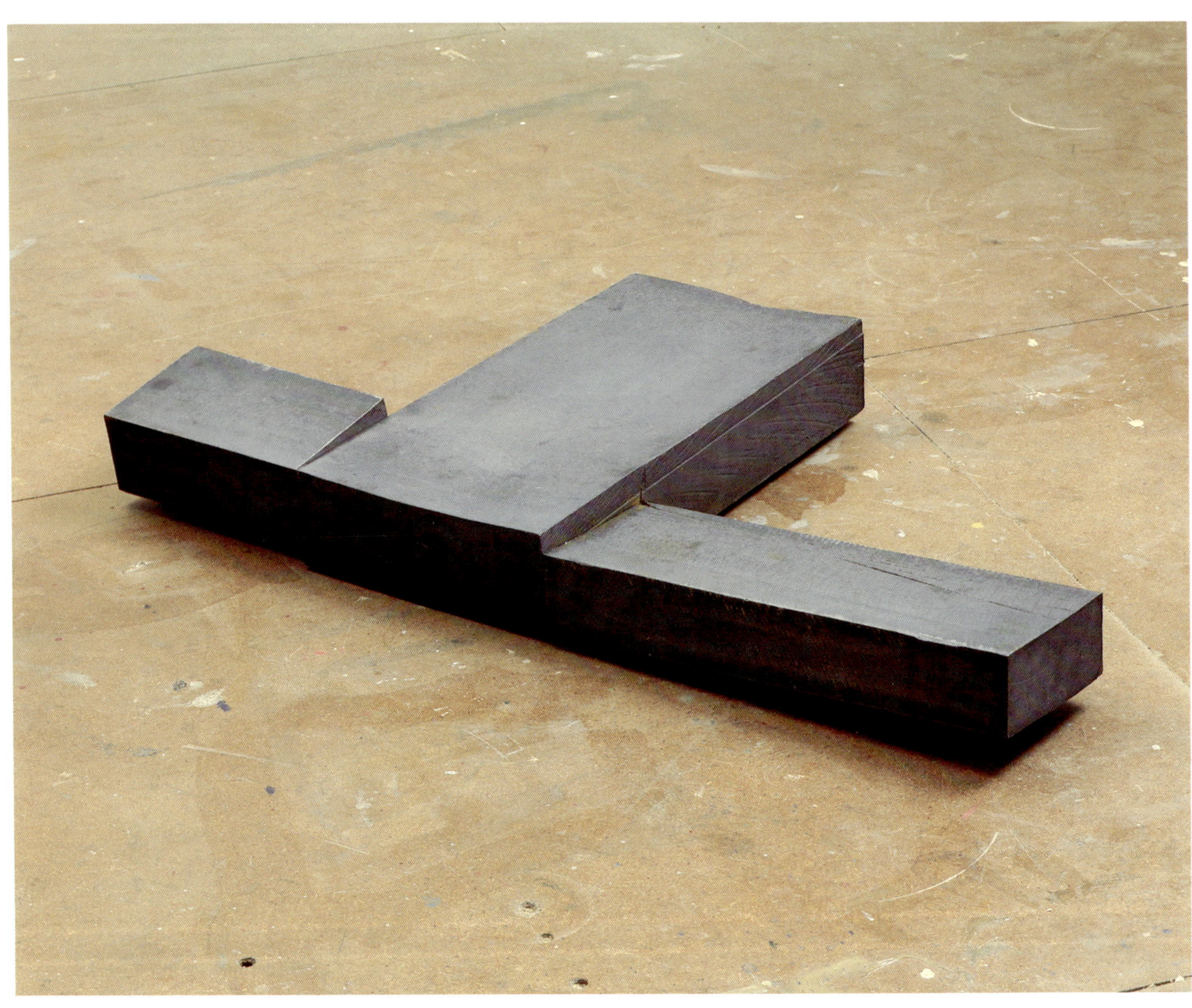

Fig. 5   Untitled, 1984
cast iron
5¼ x 24¼ x 41¾″
Collection of the Artist

JOEL SHAPIRO AND MODERNISM

To come to terms with the work of Joel Shapiro, one must address the issue of Modernism. By Modernism we mean the dominant twentieth-century concern of making art which redefines the abstract language of art to produce a contemporary statement that reflects both private and public issues. When Shapiro first surfaced before the public eye in the early 1970s, his work seemed to contradict the increasing emphasis Modernism was placing on abstraction, for his work was referential. At that time, Modernism in sculpture was defined principally by Minimal Art. Since its appearance in the early 1960s, Minimalism had reduced sculpture to its absolute essence, allowing sculpture to be about only those qualities inherent in itself. Sculpture could be about space, solid, void, texture, mass, and form, for example, but it could not refer beyond itself to the daily or the universal. There could be no morals or symbols embedded in its surface, nor could the work have any psychological presence. Characteristic of Minimal sculpture are the metal plate works conceived by Carl Andre in the late 1960s. Executed in zinc, lead, iron, or copper, for example, they consisted of 144 plates, each 12 inches by 12 inches, and ⅜ of an inch thick, laying flat on the floor to make up a square 12 feet by 12 feet. The work was about the color, texture, weight, and shape of the plates, and about the relationship of the plates to one another and the whole, and of the whole to the surrounding room. There was no moral, no metaphor, no reference of any kind within the work. The presentation was literal; what you *saw* was what you got, namely this object and your relationship to it.

The genius of Shapiro's sculpture was to reintroduce reference into art. By doing so he extended the Modernist tradition just at the very point when it seemed to dead-end by reducing itself to a highly restricted vocabulary. Most important, however, was the fact that the presence of the referential component was never clear. The viewer was challenged to read the sculpture simultaneously as abstraction and figuration without knowing for sure which of these two qualities was the thrust of the work, or how the one informed the other—if any such relationship did indeed exist. In effect, Shapiro was presenting an irony, and with that irony, a tension which gave his work a disturbing psychological presence.

Shapiro did not limit the irony and its concommitant tension to just the friction between abstraction and figuration. Rather, it is present in almost every issue that can be found in his work. Epitomizing the depth of this irony is the fact that Shapiro's sculpture seems utterly simplistic and minimal; and yet it is layered with such formal and referential richness that it lends itself to almost endless reading and re-reading.

Despite their simplicity it was immediately apparent that Shapiro's block-like house forms from the early to mid-1970s could not be read as quickly as a Minimal sculpture, which they certainly resembled. A good example is the Ringling Museum's untitled sculpture from 1975 (fig. 7), which appears at first glance to be nothing more than a cast-iron brick. But upon moving around the work, the viewer discovers that two of its sides contain small, rectangular voids. These can be read as part of the formalist play of shape against shape or mass against void. Eventually, however, the viewer thinks "house" when looking at this monolithic block, for the voids read too much like windows, although it is not possible to interpret them as such without some hesitation. Even the meaning of this "house" contains an ironic ambiguity, for this fortress-like mass can be interpreted simultaneously as protective and sheltering or as ominous and threatening. The scale of the sculpture is also filled with contradictions. Designed to sit alone in an open area, the object commands a vast amount of space, thus extending the presence of the work well beyond its actual size. The sculpture is oddly toy-like because of its diminutive scale, and especially because of its tiny "windows"; nonetheless, the work asserts a monumental presence because of the way it aggressively dominates the surrounding space. The incongruous scale of this sculpture for the real house it implies increases the disquieting tension of this work. This tiny house is clearly symbolic, although its specific meaning is never clear. The openings in this dense, little block seem to release innumerable associations, experiences, and memories that Shapiro has magically poured into the mold when casting the work.

To understand Shapiro's contribution to Modernism, we need only compare his "houses" to the work of Constantin Brancusi, who furthered the development of Modernism in the early twentieth century by abstracting representational objects to their essential geometric forms. A fine example of this process is Brancusi's *Sleeping Muse* of 1909-10 in the Hirshhorn Museum and Sculpture Garden, which is nothing more than a marble ovoid transformed into a sleeping head by elegant sweeping lines to give the suggestion of eyes, nose, and mouth. Unlike Shapiro's sculpture, there is nothing ambiguous about what is represented; Brancusi's form is unmistakably a head. Furthermore, the abstraction clearly supports the

representational component. Finally, the scale is appropriate to the object represented, and the sculpture fits comfortably in its surrounding space.

The psychological and physical tension Shapiro injected into twentieth-century abstraction redefined sculpture in the '70s and established a precedent for much of the art of the last ten years which has concentrated on representational issues and disturbing emotional states. Shapiro's own work has continued to evolve, so that his sculpture of the '80s stands in marked contrast to that of the '70s. An important, although certainly not exclusive, theme for Shapiro in the '70s was the house, which he presented in any number of guises, more often than not with a monolithic quality that could be traced back to Minimal Art. Since roughly 1980, Shapiro has explored the theme of the figure, and has done so more exclusively than he did the house, or any other theme, in the preceding decade. The figure, of course, is a natural extension of the house motif, which in actuality functioned as a metaphor for the human condition. It is therefore not surprising to discover that the figure first made its appearance in Shapiro's art in 1973, although not until the late '70s did it appear with any regularity.

More important, the style of Shapiro's work changed toward 1980 when the figure emerged as a clear and definite theme. Shapiro purged his sculpture of Minimalism's monolithic structure and architectural space as he gradually began working with a constructivist vocabulary of joining together geometric blocks and planes, often in complicated compositions. The recent work has become increasingly tense, energetic, and filled with implicit movement. Furthermore, the scale of the work has grown, to the point that a bronze, cast in June of 1986, measures fourteen feet in height. Small scale work has virtually been abandoned, and with it Shapiro's preoccupation with defining architectural space.

Despite his stylistic and thematic evolution, Shapiro's work is still predicated on the same issues of ambiguity and irony that made his work of the '70s so successful. Now, however, the tension has been increased by the complexity of the compositions. Many of the works, such as the 1982-83 untitled bronze in the artist's collection (fig. 10), appear to have a box or plank torso which acts as a fulcrum from which project beam "arms," "legs," "heads," or "necks." The entire composition is off-axis, for none of these architectural parts is horizontal or vertical. Adding to the constantly shifting quality of the work is the way in which the various parts of the composition are put together, for they are joined at peculiar angles that work against the implied geometry of the individual planks or beams. The disparity in the length of the appendages also increases the staccato rhythm of the piece. This same staccato pace is set up in the relationship of the viewer to the work. Just as the sculpture has no horizontal or vertical axiality, it also has no primary axis for the viewer to approach it, in the sense that it has no front or back. Instead the work, which is intended to be seen in the round, consists of a number of different compositions and viewpoints that abruptly arrest the viewer as they demand to be read and analyzed.

As was the case with the works from the '70s, there is an ironic ambiguity fueling the tension of the recent sculpture. Any one reading is countered by its exact opposite. The most obvious irony, which dates back to the '70s, is the dual reading of the work as abstraction and figuration. If read as abstraction, there is the issue of seeing those works as asymmetrical and energetic, defying compositional logic and even gravity; and yet

they are wonderfully balanced, even if quite precariously. Ironically, many of these sculptures, while compositionally balanced, are not actually stable and instead rely on bolts in the floor to keep them upright! Certainly the works look light, as the beams seem to spin like weightless sticks around their fulcrum, but in reality the cast-iron and cast-bronze works are extremely heavy. The works can seem cold and geometric; nevertheless, the surfaces of many of the beams and planks are warm and feel handmade, revealing the artist's personal touch as he worked the wood, a quality that is retained in the cast sculptures as well. Paradoxically, these cast works look Constructivist—as if made from a number of planar parts that have been pieced together— whereas the sculpture really exists as a single unit. And, as mentioned above, there is the irony of the composition, which, in effect, is redefined as the viewer moves around the work.

Every attempt to attach a narrative to the figurative element of these sculptures likewise results in contradictory interpretations. On the one hand, these figures seem to be graceful or playful, while, on the other hand, they are frightening and in some respects hysterical, for these truncated forms seem to be on the brink of collapsing or flying apart. In the Exxon Corporation's untitled bronze of 1981-84 (fig. 11), the figure can be read as thrusting upward just as readily as it can be seen as tumbling. The figure in the untitled bronze from 1985 (fig. 13) can be seen as descending as if to do a split or as ascending as if straining to raise itself. It is impossible to determine whether figures are rising or falling since the top can be read as the bottom just as easily as an "arm" can be seen as a "leg" or a "head."

This ironic ambiguity and its accompanying disturbing psychology are precisely what

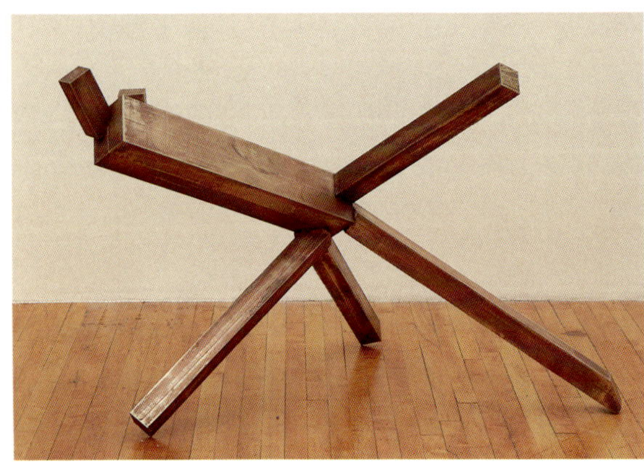

Fig. 6   Untitled, 1985
bronze   A.P.
36¼ x 53 x 40"
Collection of the Artist

distinguishes Shapiro's sculpture from that of
his many Modernist forerunners, such as the
Russian Constructivists or, more recently, the
American, David Smith. Certainly a number
of parallels exist between Shapiro and his
predecessors. Take for example the welded
steel sculptures from Smith's famous *Cubi*
series of the early 1960s. These works use a
Constructivist vocabulary of attaching in an
additive process geometric units to one
another and a central post. The *Cubi*
sculptures are even totemic and haunting,
containing a primeval spirit which is a vestige
of Smith's upbringing in Surrealism. And, yet,
there is neither tension nor ambiguity in
Smith's work, which is clearly stated by the
very fact that, in direct contrast to Shapiro, he
aligned his work in vertical and horizontal
axes, thus presenting a logic and order that
renders the primeval mystery almost peaceful
and soothing. Nor is there any tension
between abstraction and the figuration; the
work is very definitely first about formal
relationships. An anthropomorphic reading of
the sculpture is secondary, although it is
certainly not without meaning, since the
human presence seems to lurk beneath the
surface of the work and thus functions like a
spector haunting the elemental world Smith
has created.

Several of Shapiro's recent sculptures
included in this exhibition are totemic and
monolithic and thus stand in marked contrast
to most of his other work from this period.
The 1983-84 untitled bronze in the collection
of the Newark Museum (fig. 9) and the 1985
bronze in the collection of the artist (fig. 3)
are vertical and still, working with gravity and
the horizontality of the floor rather than trying
to deny either. These stolid figures defiantly
hold their ground and reign supreme like the
carved deities of a primitive culture. The
Newark Museum bronze bears a particularly
strong resemblance to many kinds of African
carvings which rely so heavily on frontality
and a minimal, ideographic vocabulary to
invest the materials with a mystical presence.
Tension yields some ground to mystery as
Shapiro concentrates on the shamanistic
powers of sculpture. In many respects, the
aura surrounding these works is similar to that
in his monolithic houses from the '70s, which
had a dream-like, mysterious quality that
elicited a range of associations from the
viewer.

Shapiro's drawings from the '80s retain a
greater degree of this mystery than do the
tense, Constructivist sculptures, to which they
often relate. Working with bold, dark forms in
charcoal, Shapiro captures the weight and
presence of the metal of his sculpture. The
relationship of the forms and the space
between them is not unlike that found in his
three-dimensional work. But through the
smudging of the charcoal, the dramatic value
contrast of light and dark, and the vast,
illusionistic space that can only be created in a
two-dimensional medium, Shapiro has
endowed these drawings with a potent drama
which verges on the romantic sublime. In
particular, the primal drama of Abstract
Expressionism comes to mind; the value
contrast of dark form against a light ground
recalls Franz Kline, while the specks of

charcoal floating in the open space function
similarly, despite their very different look, to
the small patches of paint that Clyfford Still
left isolated in his vast sea of color. The
cropping of form by the edge of the paper to
suggest an infinite space beyond the actual
drawing, as well as the emphasis on process—
the smudging and trailing of the charcoal—
which records the artist's personal work, are
other devices that bring to mind Abstract
Expressionism. Many of these qualities,
including a mysterious aura, could be found in
Shapiro's work from the '70s, and the
drawings are therefore very much a natural
extension of Shapiro's sculpture, although
they are never studies per se for them.

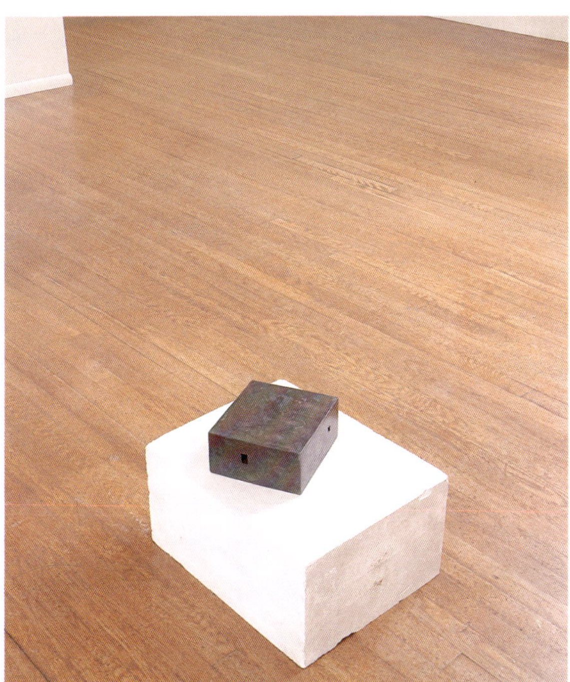

Actually, the recent drawings are what the
sculptures could never be; because of the
illusionistic properties of the medium, they
are able to make explicit the implicit
movement and energy of the three-
dimensional work. If the sculptures *looked* like
they were on the verge of exploding or
imploding, the forms in the drawings actually
are, as is readily evident in the Quinn
collection charcoal (fig. 18) where an "arm"
has split off a torso, its separation made all the
more dramatic by the cloud of charcoal dust
and smears engulfing it.

As was the case with the sculpture,
however, ironic ambiguity rules the medium.
Scale, form, and meaning are continually
subject to contradictory interpretations. Many
of the drawings, such as the one in the
collection of the Museum of Contemporary
Art, Los Angeles (fig. 24) and a second lent
courtesy of the Paula Cooper Gallery (fig. 17),
can be read in terms of abstraction or
figuration. When seen as abstract form, the
space appears vast, as in a Kandinsky
abstraction from the '30s, for example. When
the form is read as a figure, however, a human
scale is imposed on the composition, so that
what was vast and indeterminate suddenly
becomes defined and comprehensible. And
then there is the wonderful contrast of the
hard-edge, geometric, calculated forms of the
composition with the sensuous and romantic
smudging of the charcoal.

While this contrast of calculated geometry
versus emotional suspense is present in much
of Shapiro's work, central to his sculpture and
drawing is an exploration of the language of
art which forces the viewer to reconsider the
ways in which form, scale, and space can
function. It is precisely this preoccupation
with the formal properties of the medium that
places Shapiro in the Modernist tradition and
distinguishes him from his Post-Modernist
contemporaries, who in the '80s have
presented similar tension-filled,
psychologically-rich images, but images that
fail to advance the language of art as they
instead nostalgically seek refuge in the art-
historical past.

                                        M.O.

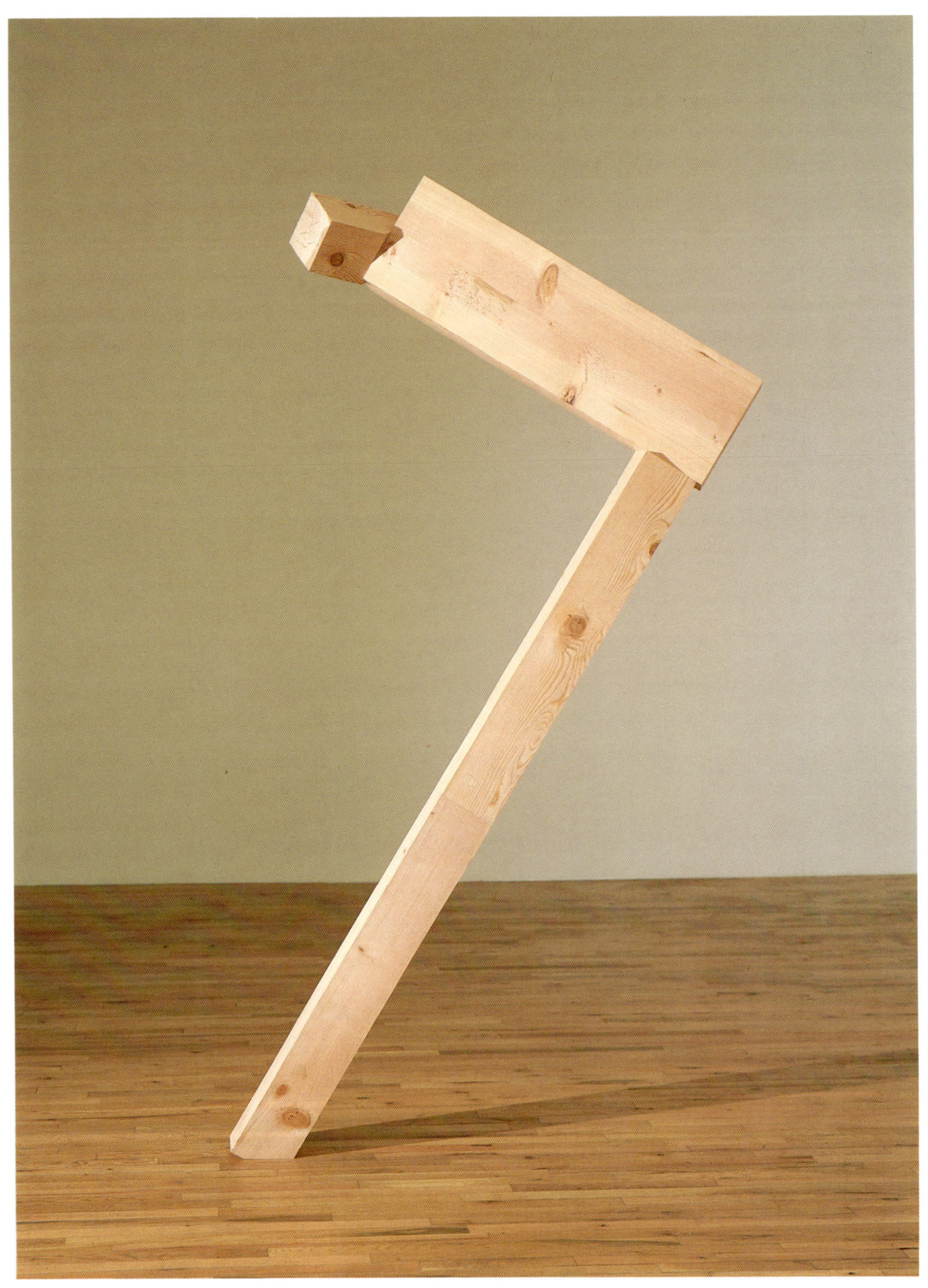

Fig. 8   Untitled, 1983
Douglas Fir
86 x 18 x 49½″
Collection of the Artist

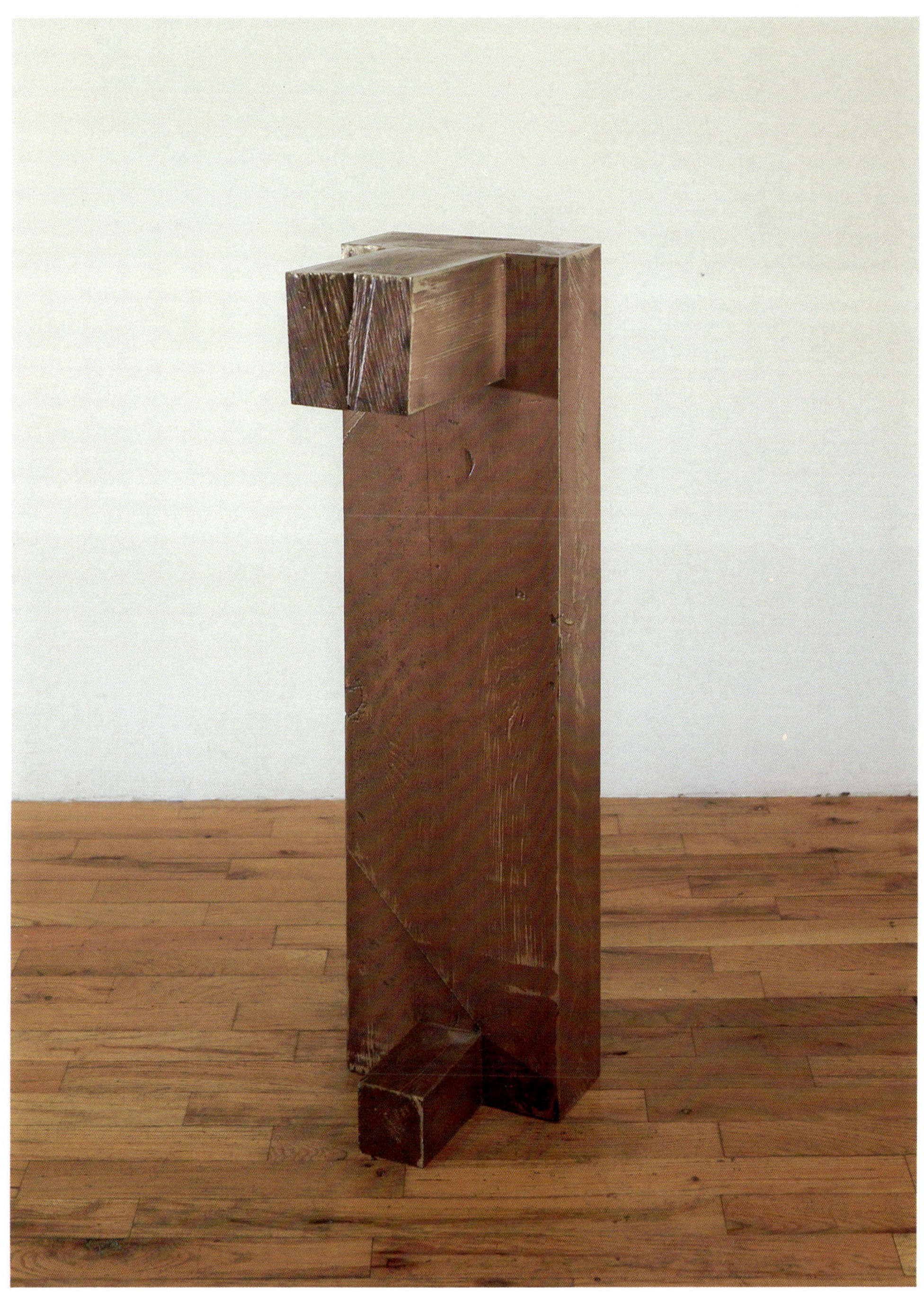

Fig. 9   Untitled, 1983-84
bronze
30 x 8½ x 11½″   1/2
The Newark Museum

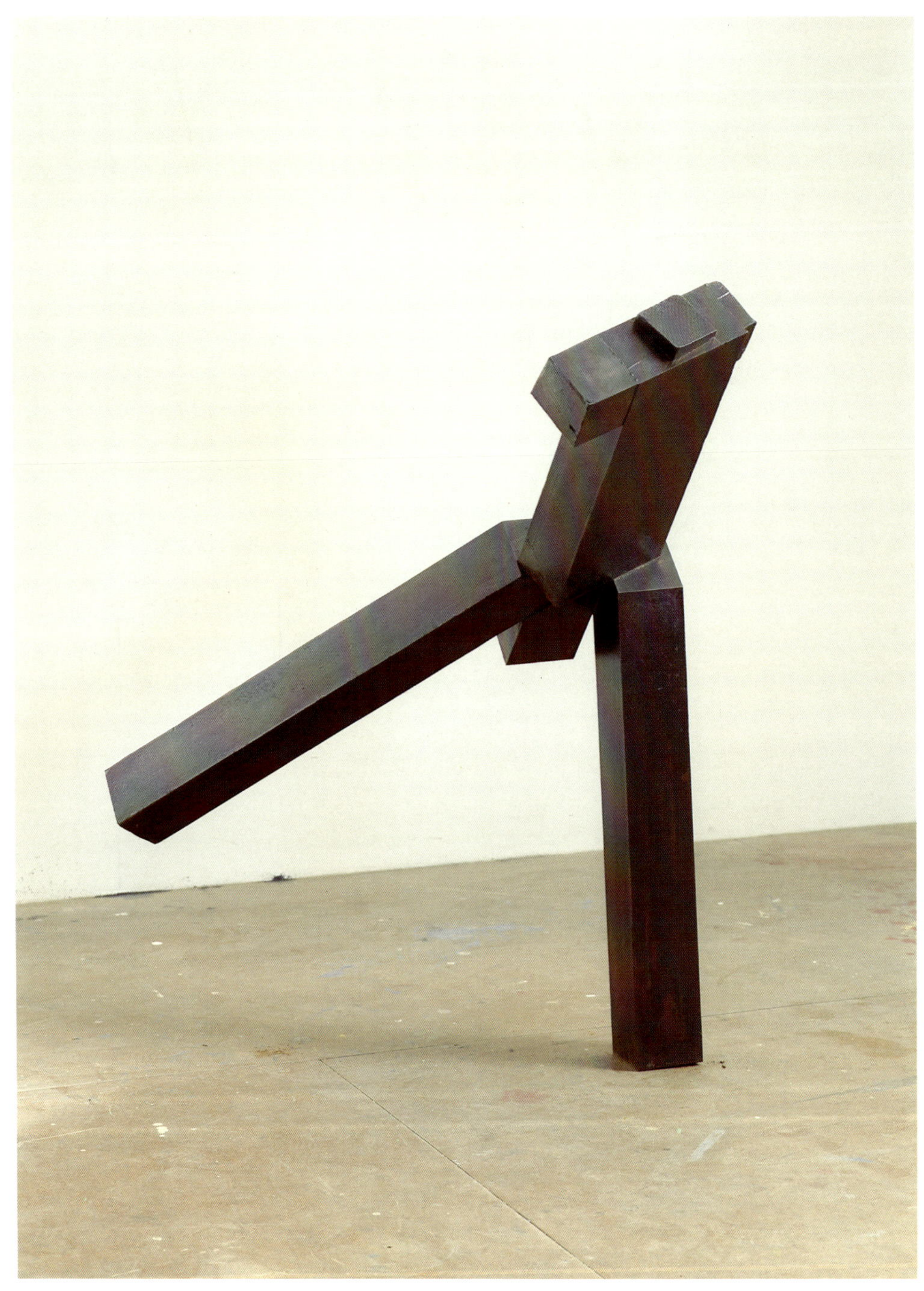

Fig. 10 Untitled, 1982-83
cast bronze   A.P.
43 x 34 x 35¾"
Collection of the Artist

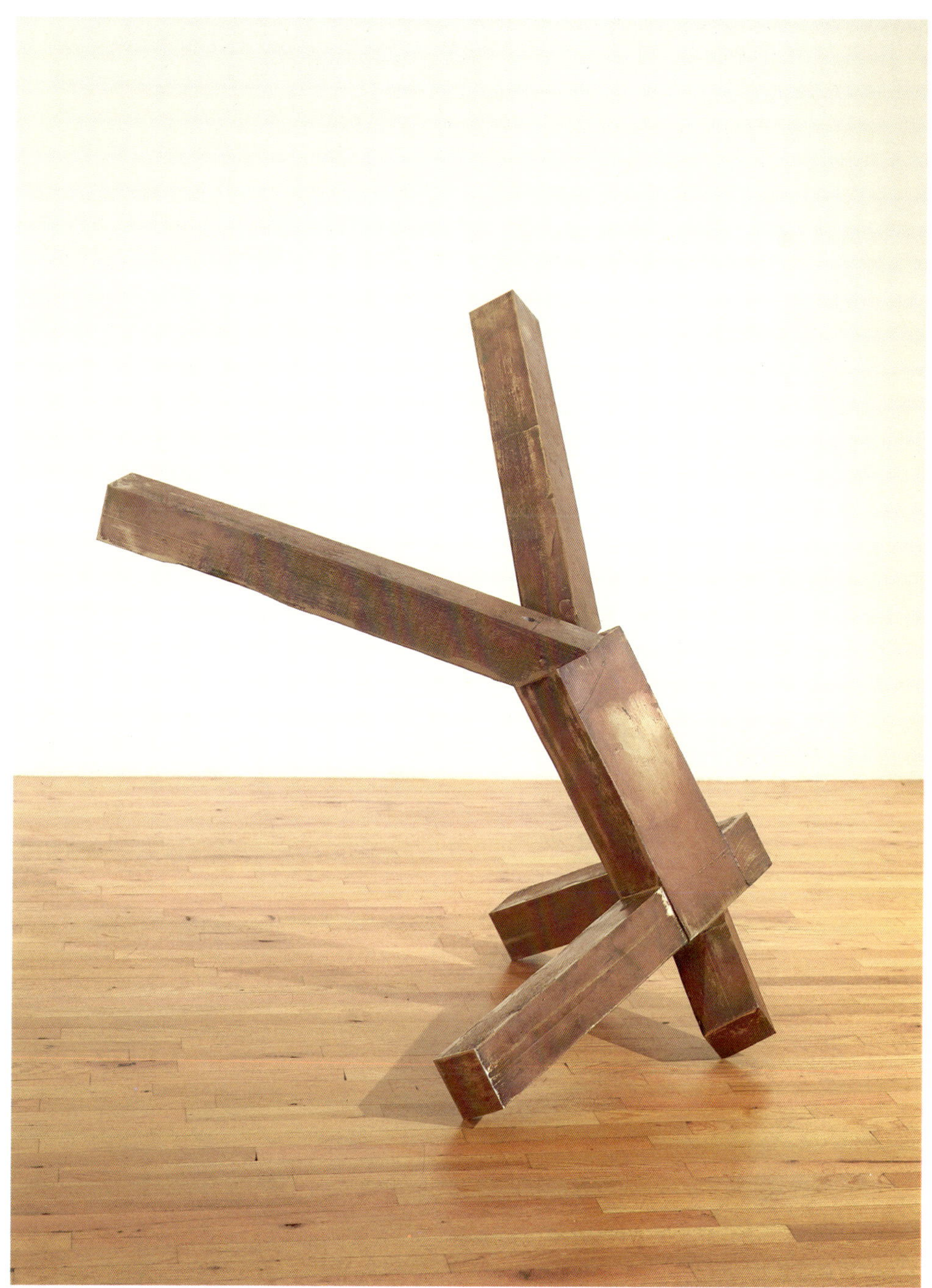

Fig. 11   Untitled, 1981-84
           bronze
           47½ x 47 x 46½″
           The Collection of Exxon Corporation

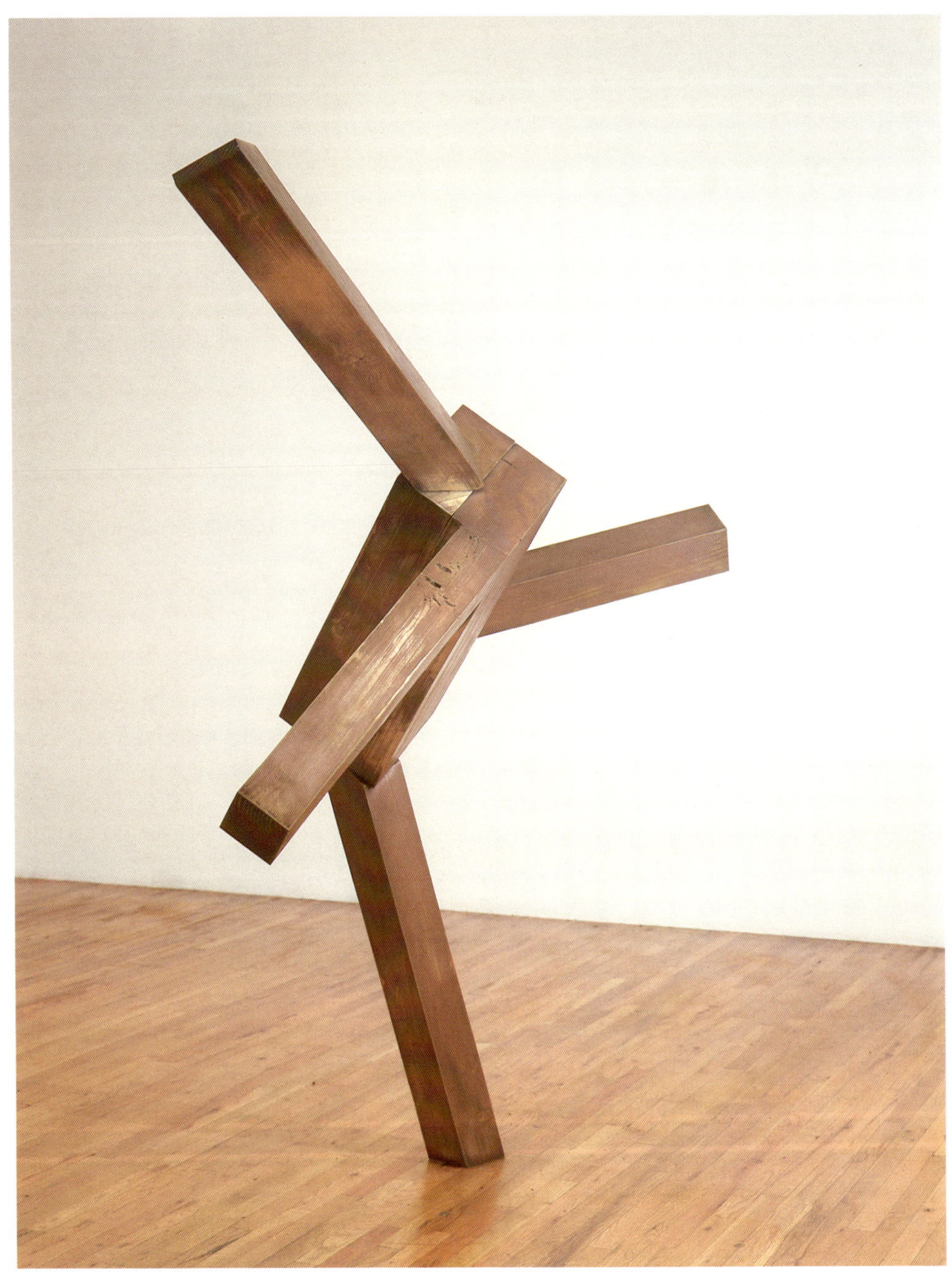

Fig. 12   Untitled, 1983-84
bronze A.P.
80¾ x 80 x 52″
Collection of the Artist

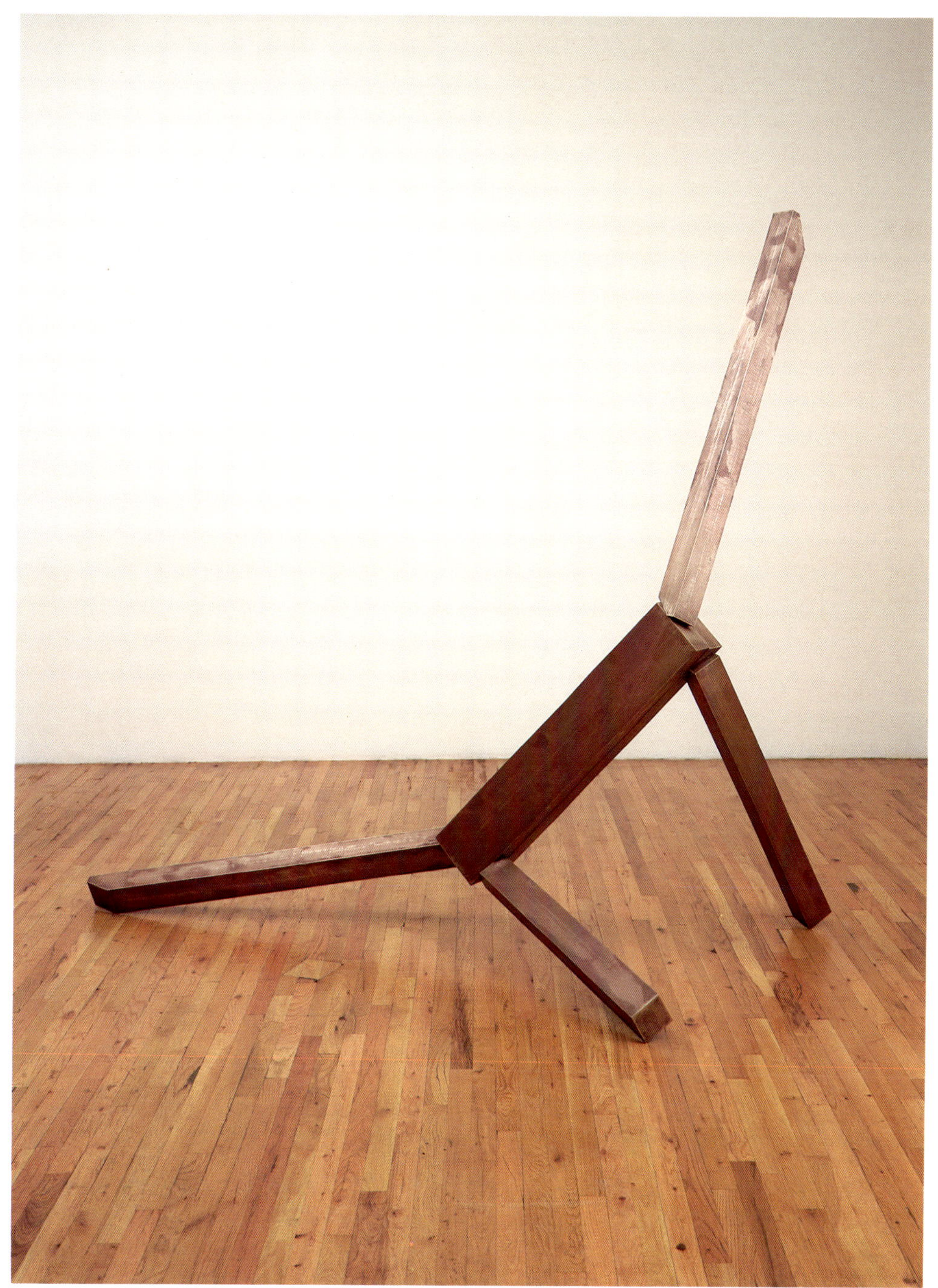

Fig. 13   Untitled, 1985
bronze   3/3
90¼ x 89¾ x 52½"
Courtesy Paula Cooper Gallery, New York

Drawings

Drawings

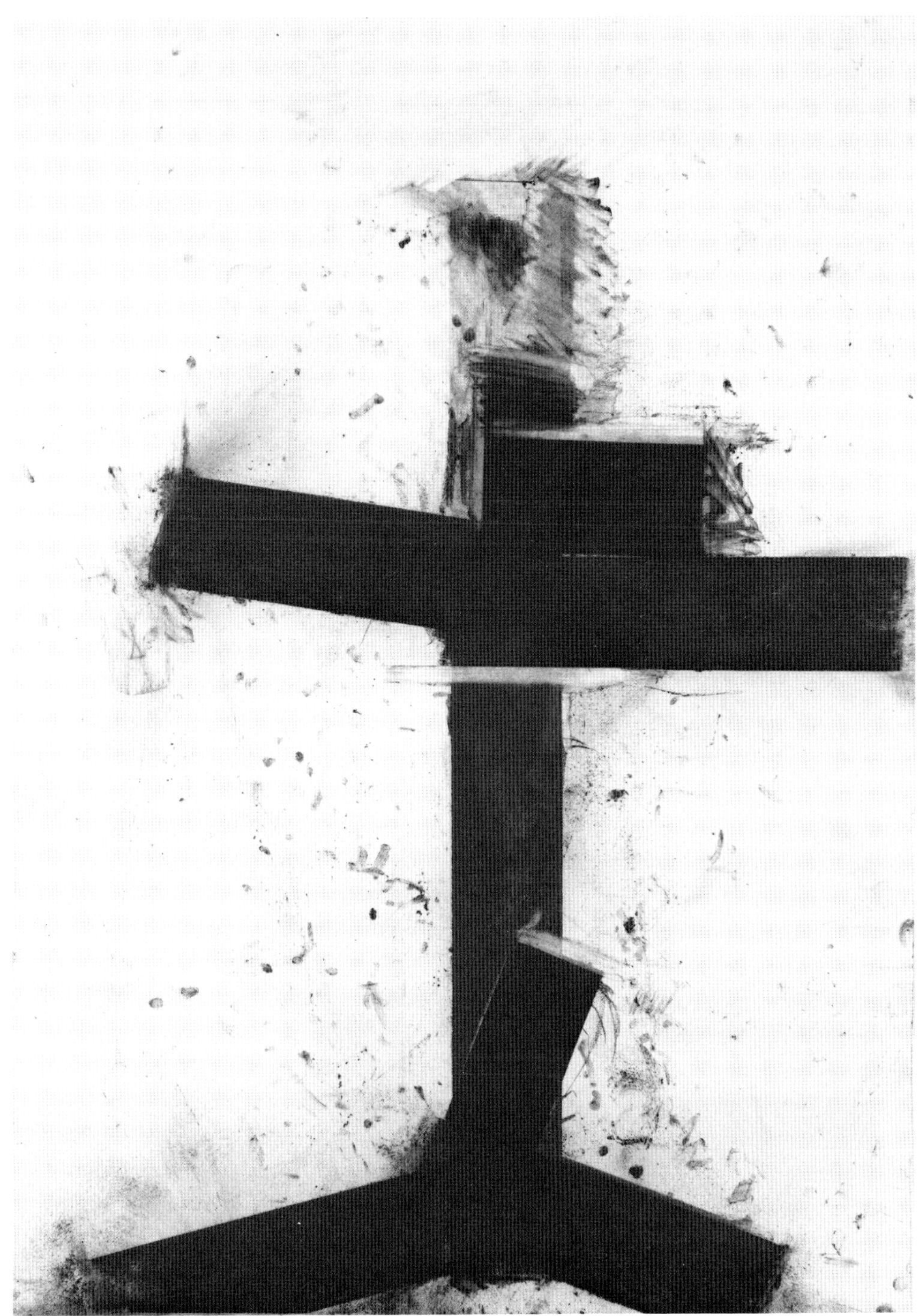

Fig. 14   Untitled 1985
           chalk and charcoal on paper
           43″ x 30¾″
           The Collection of Exxon Corporation

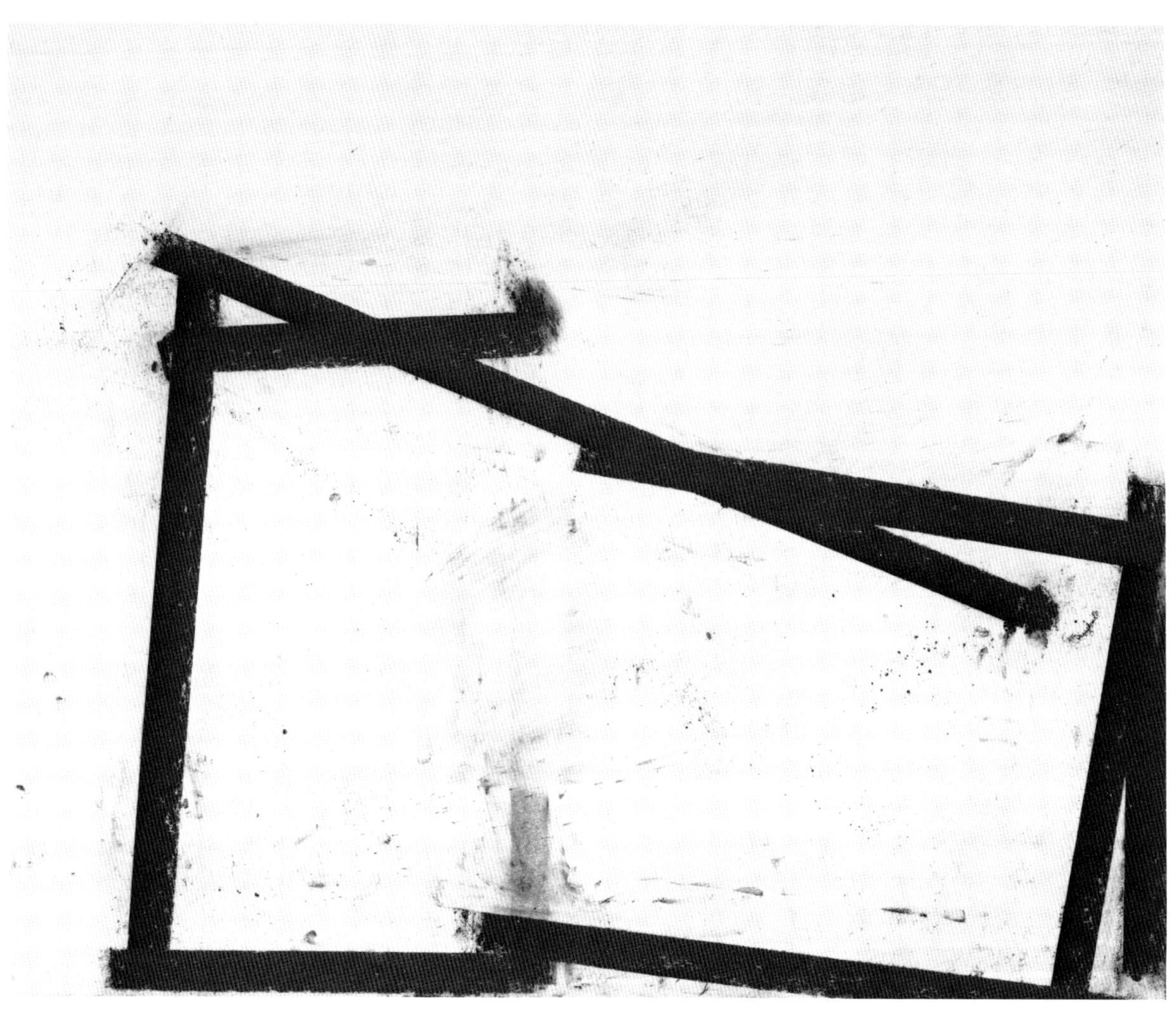

Fig. 15   Untitled, 1981
charcoal on paper
30⅛″ x 36¾″
Sophie M. Friedman Fund
Courtesy, Museum of Fine Arts, Boston

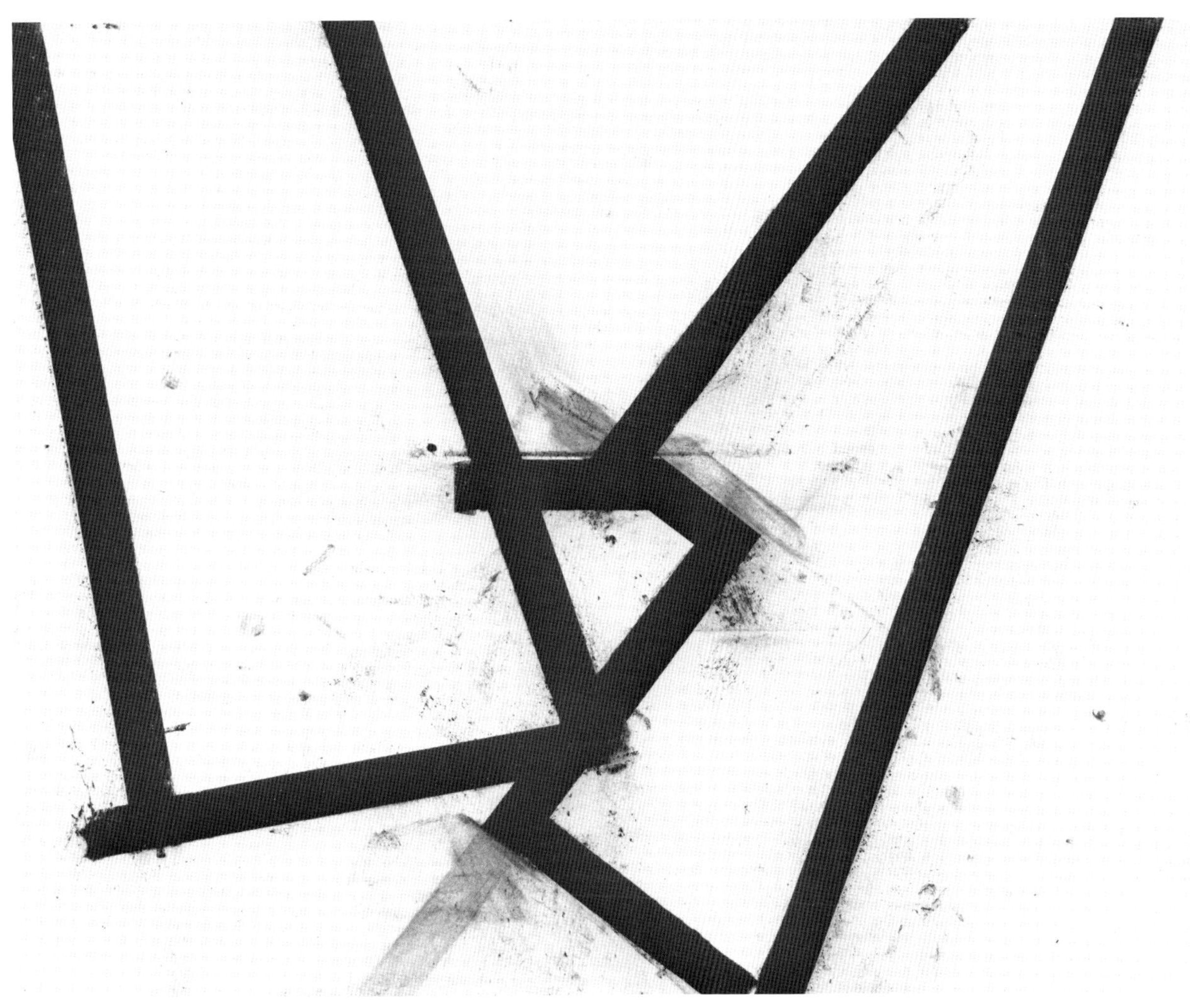

Fig. 16   Untitled, 1981
charcoal on paper
26⅛″ x 32⅜″
Gift of Laura Carpenter and Perry Bentley
Dallas Museum of Art

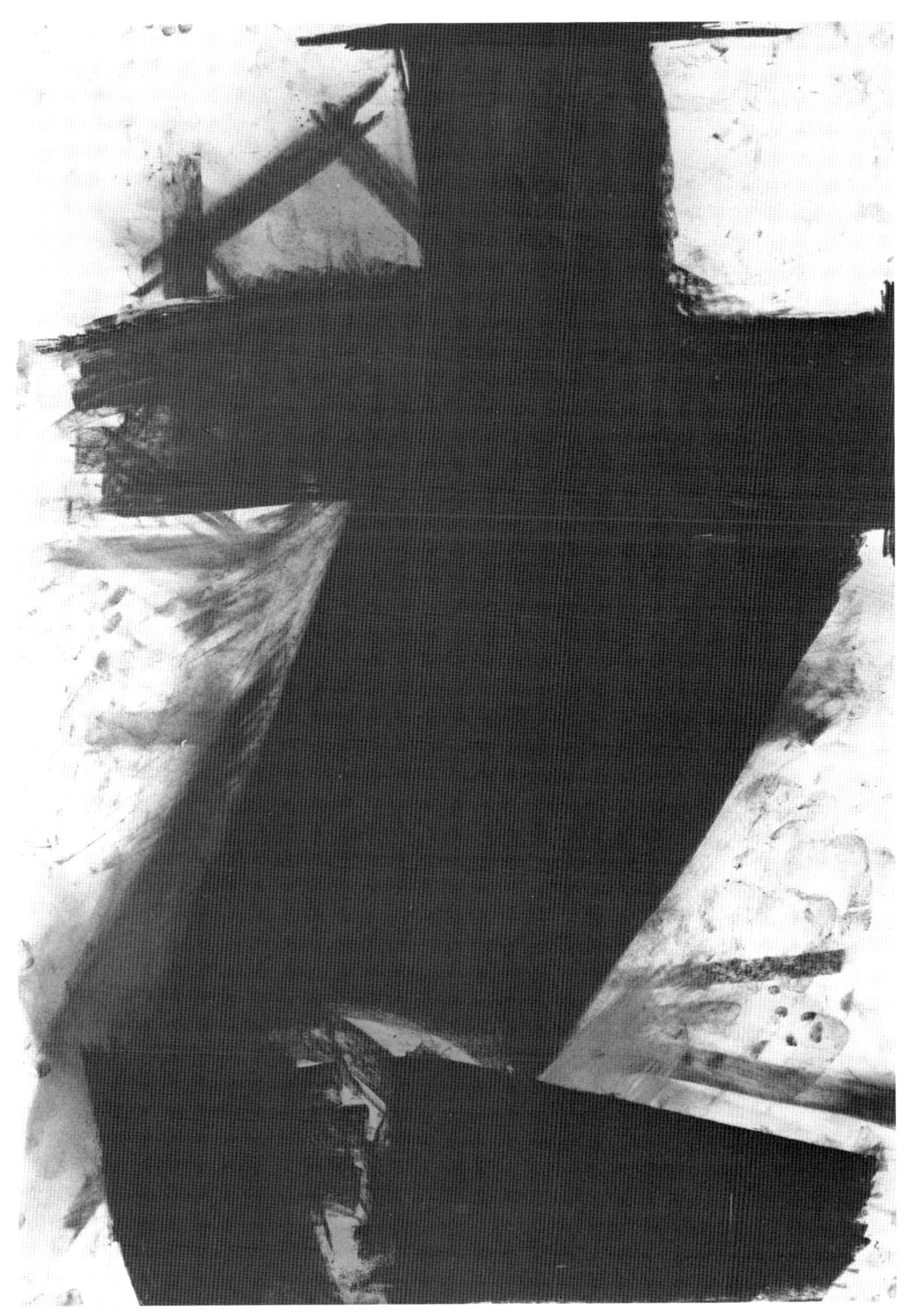

Fig. 17   Untitled, 1985
charcoal and gouache on paper
43¼″ x 30⅞″
Paula Cooper Gallery, New York

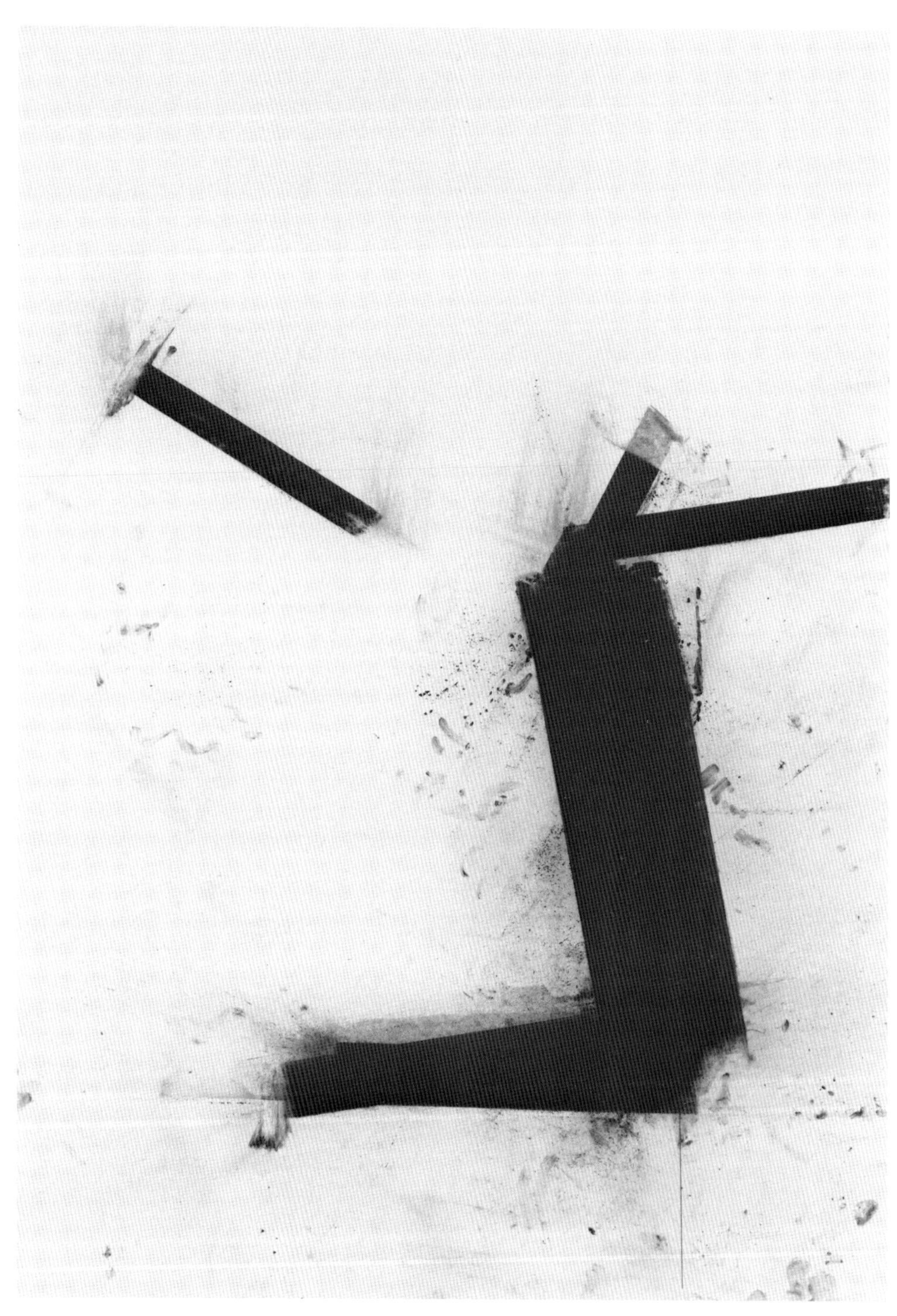

Fig. 18   Untitled, 1985
charcoal on paper
43″ x 30¾″
Collection of Mr. & Mrs. Robert Quinn

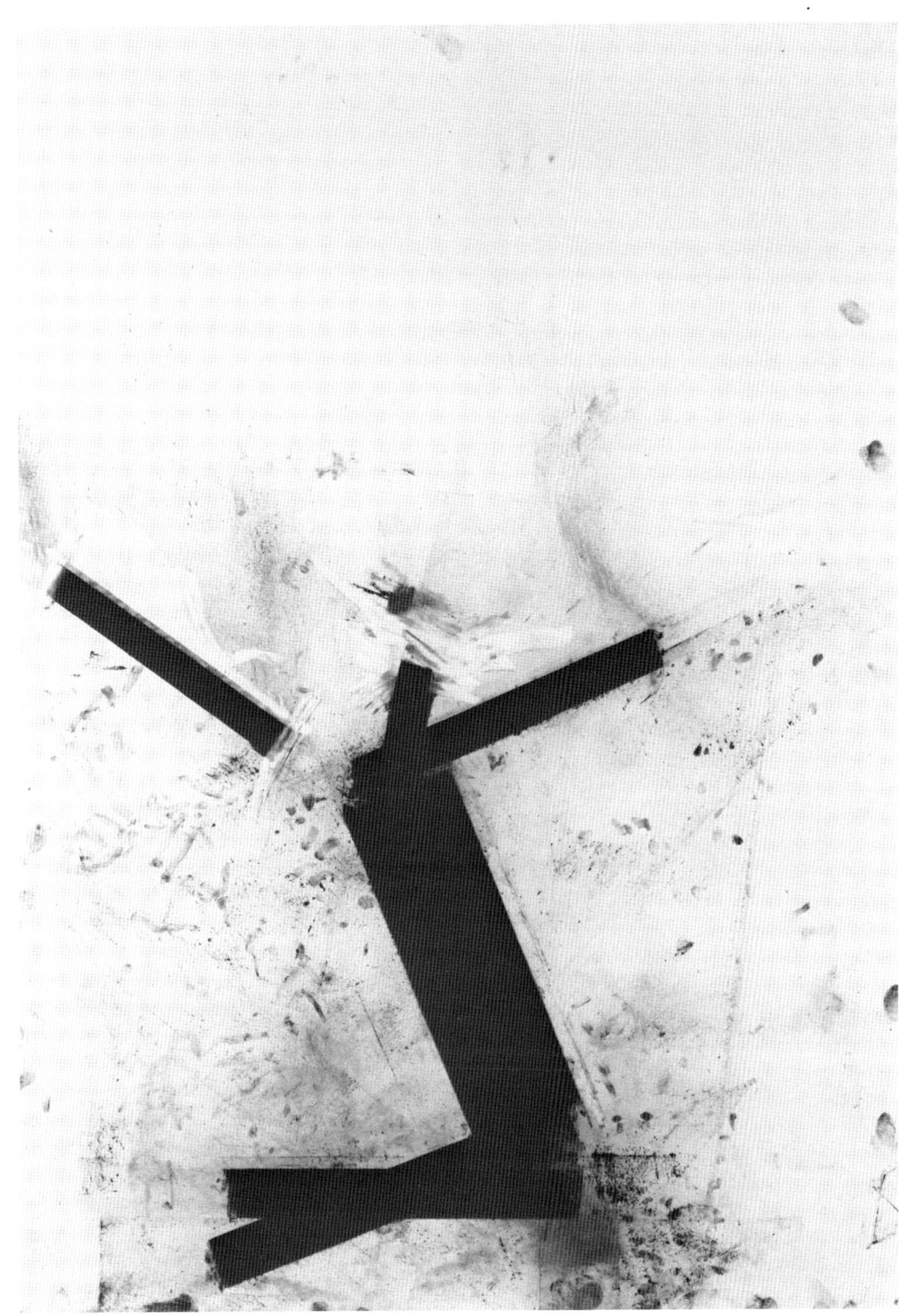

Fig. 19   Untitled, 1985
charcoal on paper
44″ x 30¾″
Keny and Johnson Gallery

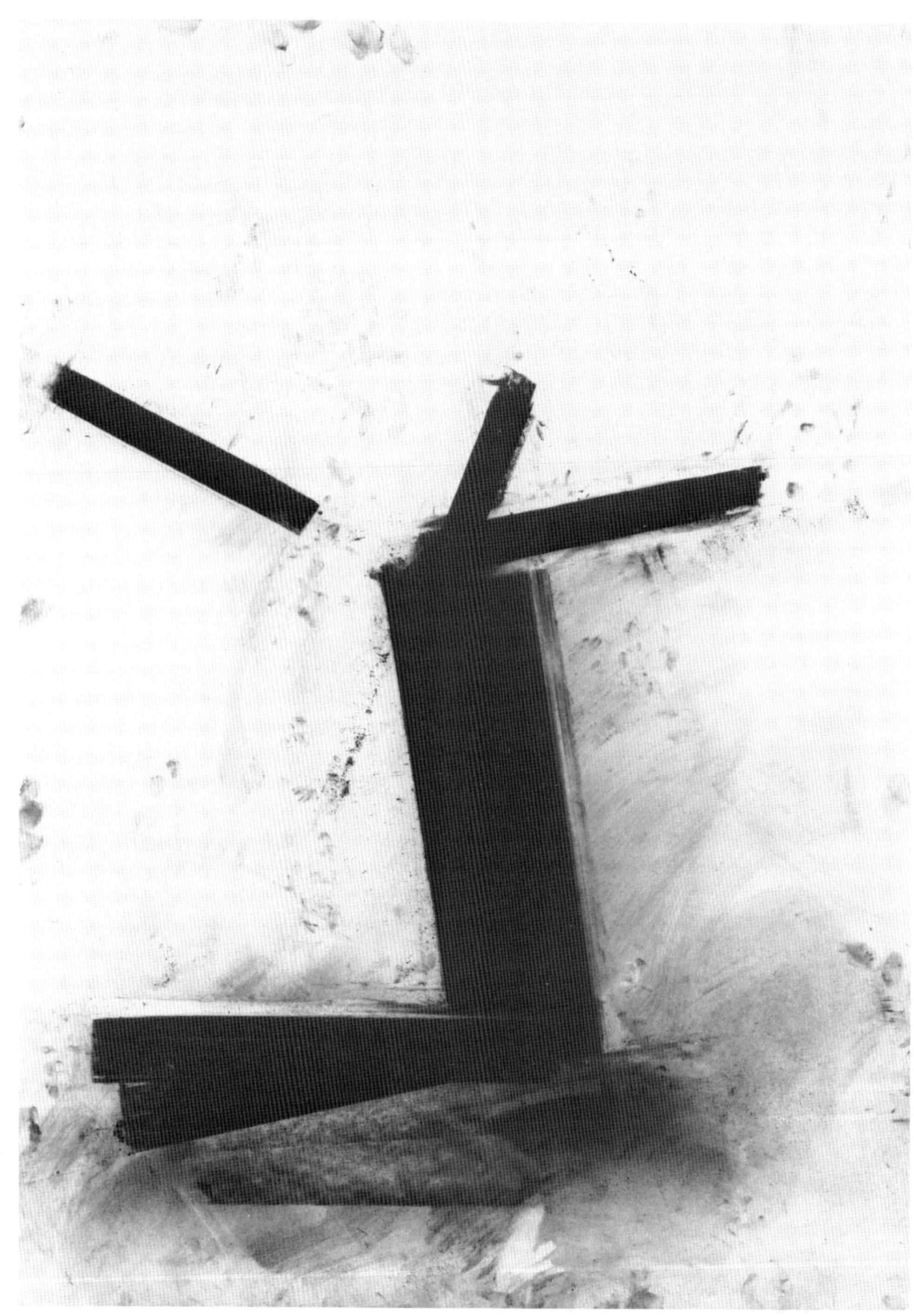

Fig. 20 Untitled, 1985
charcoal on paper
43″ x 30¾″
Collection of Mr. and Mrs. Robert Buford

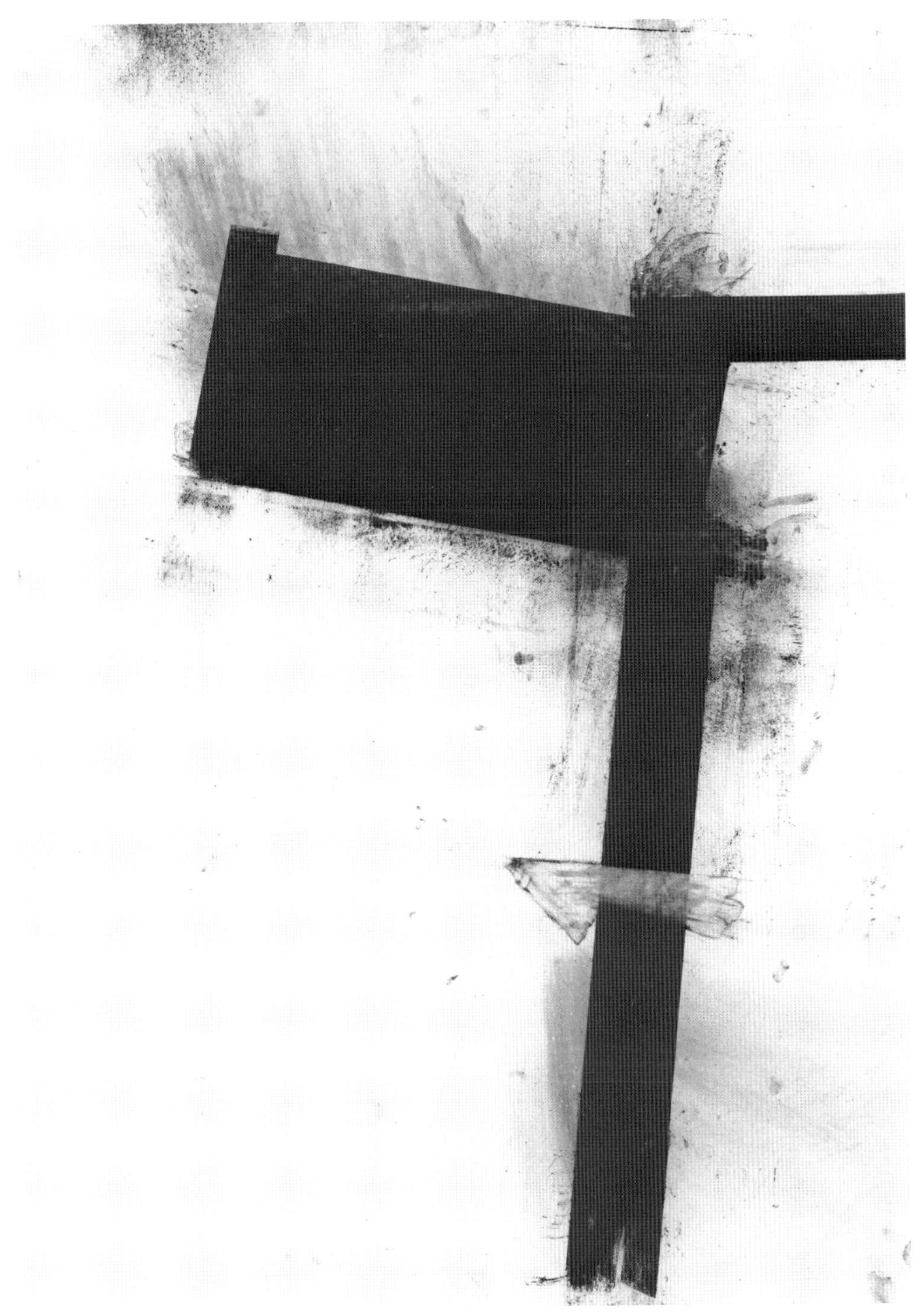

Fig. 21   Untitled, 1985
charcoal on paper
43¼″ x 30¾″
Private Collection, Boston

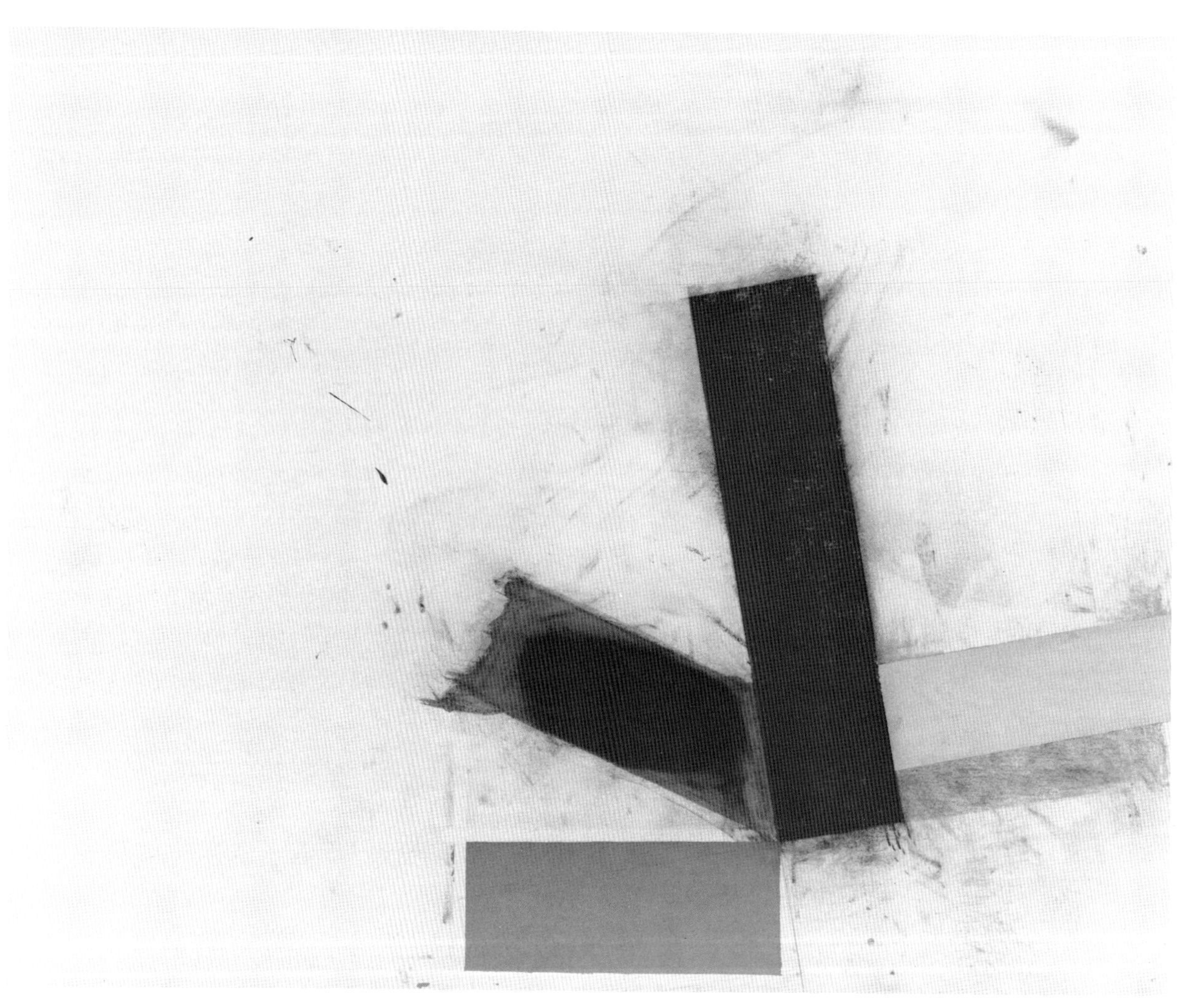

Fig. 22   Untitled, 1982-83
charcoal and gouache on paper
40½″ x 49⅞″
Mr. & Mrs. A. Skeppner

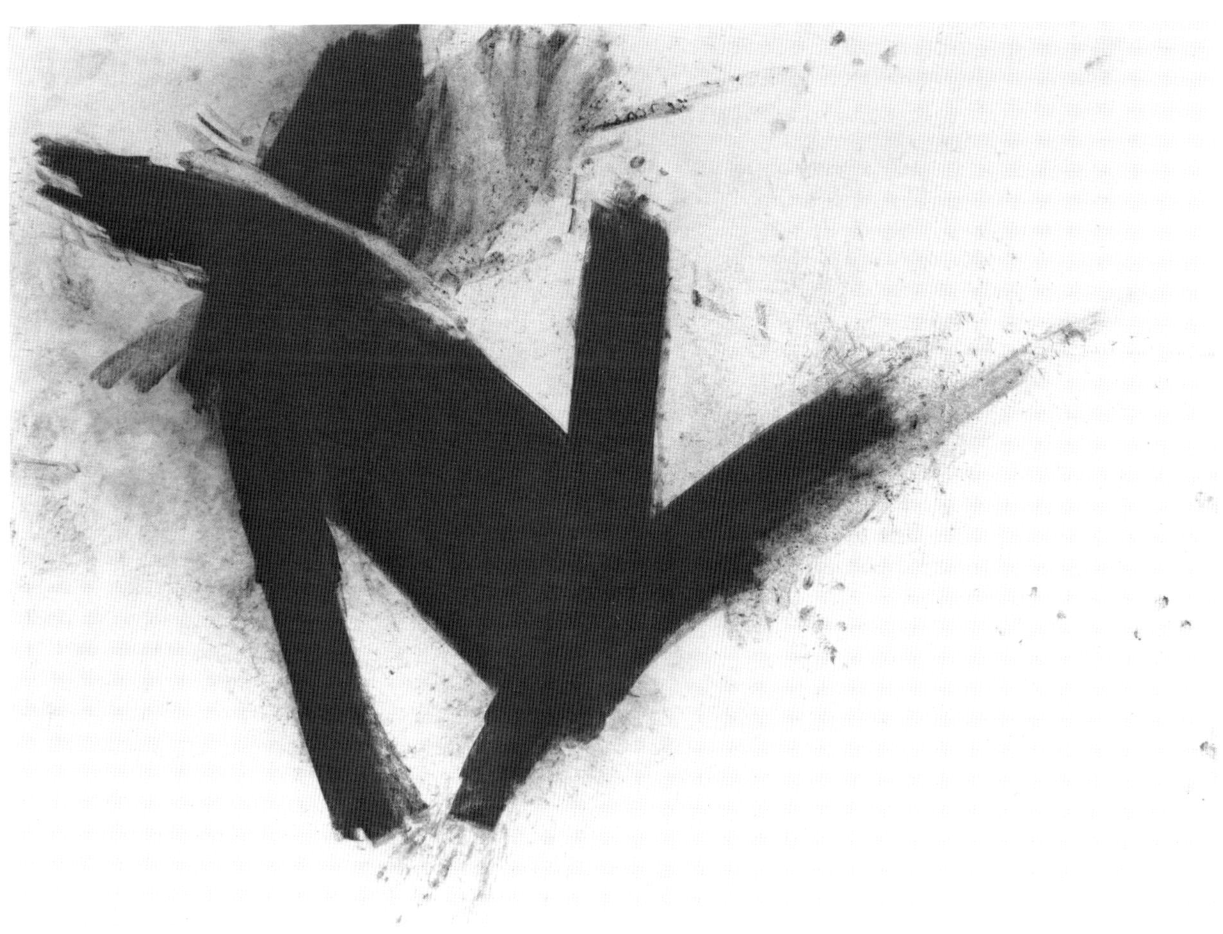

Fig. 23   Untitled, 1985
charcoal on paper
19″ x 26″
Mr. & Mrs. Gilbert Edelson

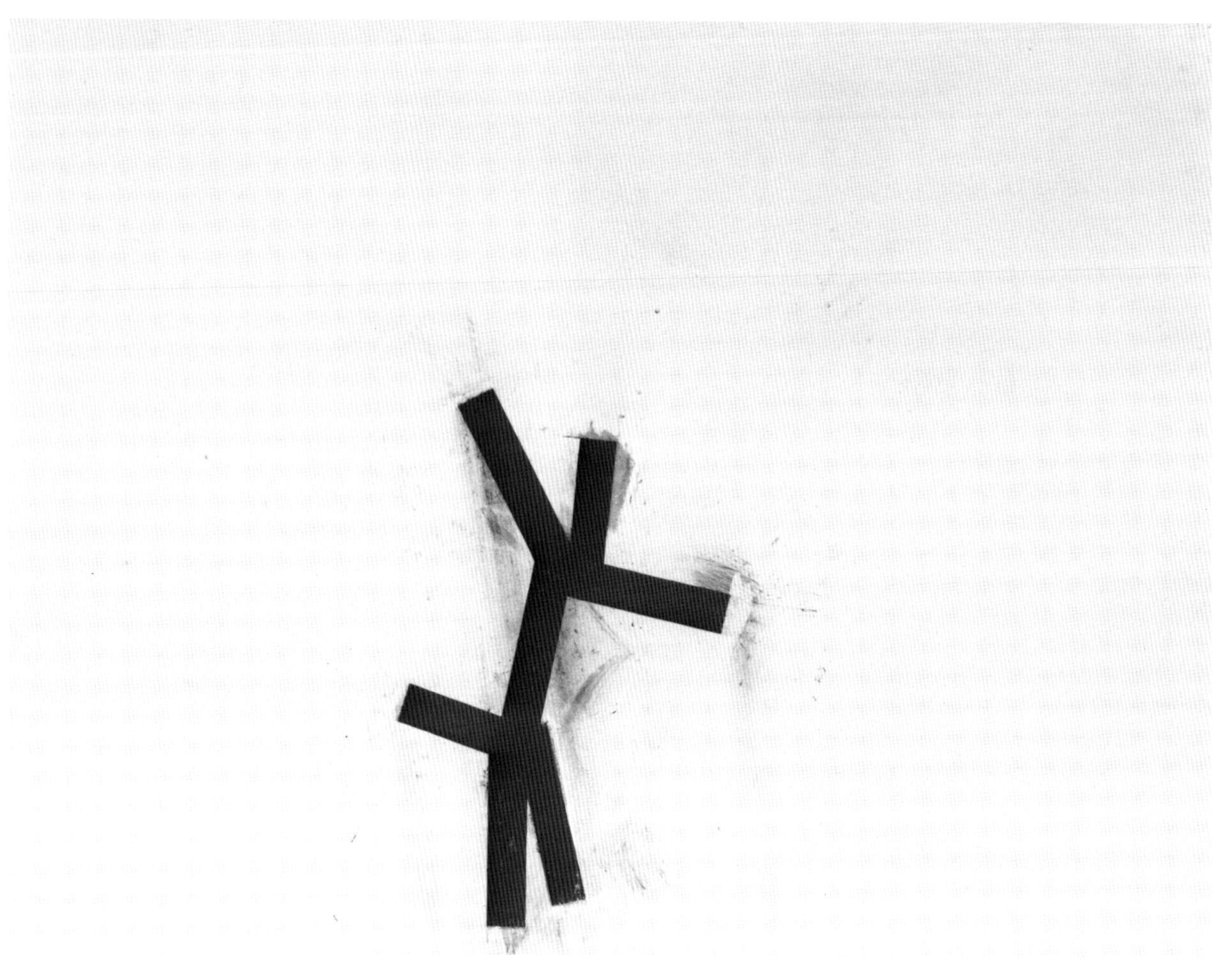

Fig. 24   Untitled, 1982
            chalk and charcoal on paper
            38″ x 50″
            The Museum of Contemporary Art, Los Angeles
            The Barry Lowen Collection

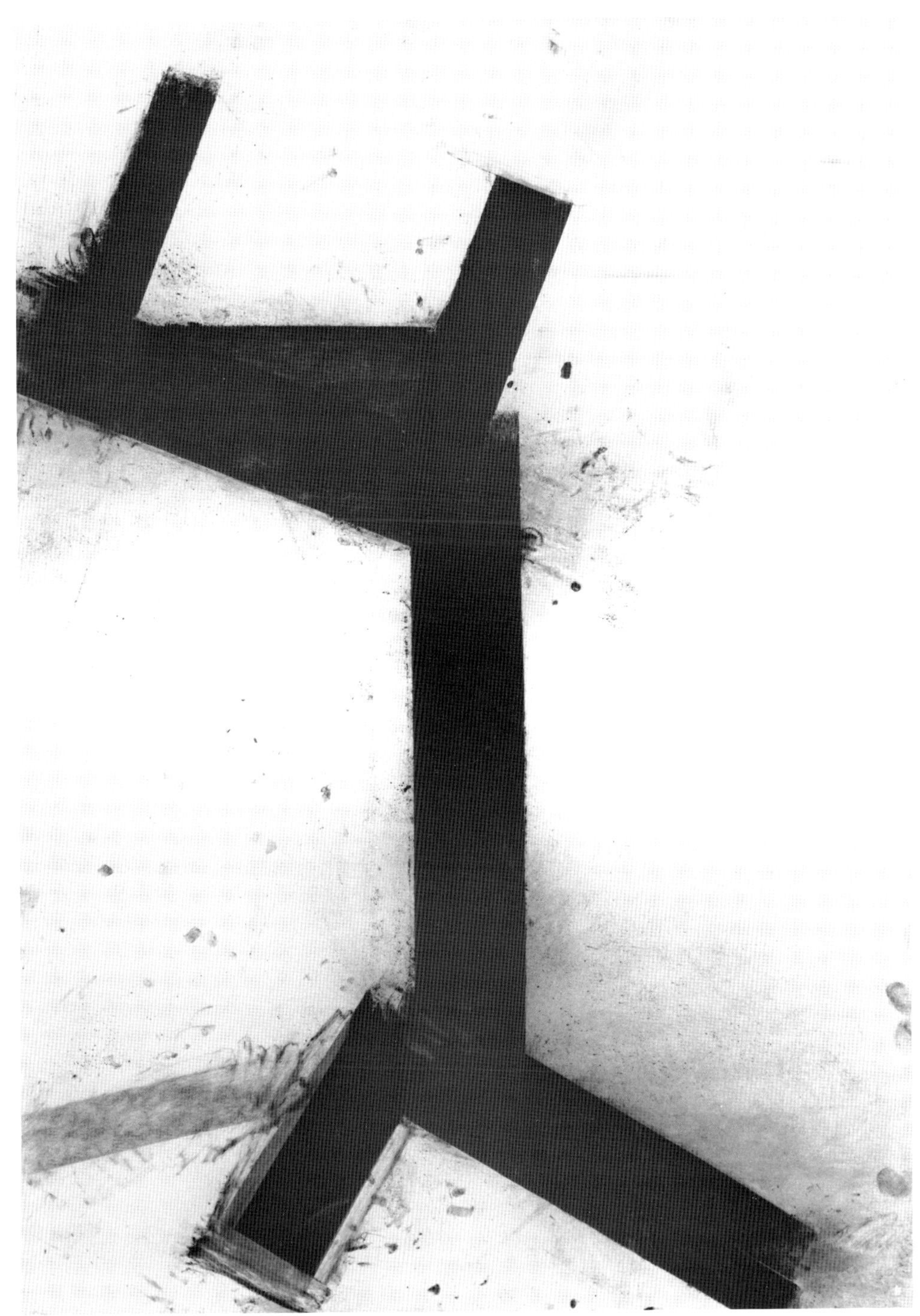

Fig. 25   Untitled, 1985
            chalk and charcoal on paper
            43″ x 30¾″
            General Mills Art Collection

BIOGRAPHY

Joel Shapiro was born in New York in 1941. He studied at New York University, B.A. 1964 and M.A. 1969. He has had several teaching positions and he has received numerous awards.

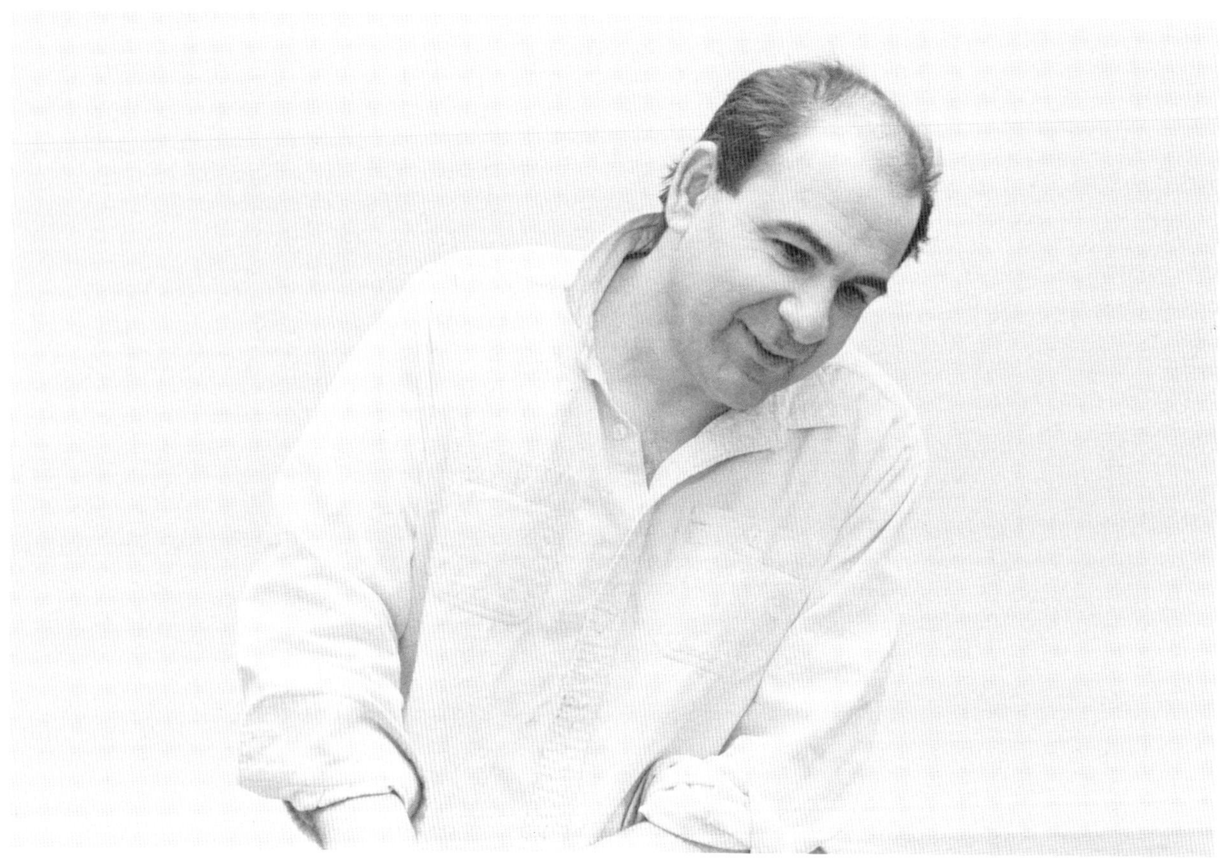

ONE-MAN EXHIBITIONS

1970	Paula Cooper Gallery, New York
1972	Paula Cooper Gallery, New York
1973	The Clocktower, Institute for Art and Urban Resources, New York
1974	Paula Cooper Gallery, New York
	Galeria Salvatore Ala, Milan
1975	The Garage, London
	Walter Kelly Gallery, Chicago
	Paula Cooper Gallery, New York
1976	Paula Cooper Gallery, Los Angeles
	Museum of Contemporary Art, Chicago
1977	Max Protetch Gallery, Washington, D.C.
	Albright-Knox Art Gallery, Buffalo
	Susanne Hilberry Gallery, Birmingham, Michigan
	Paula Cooper Gallery, New York
	Galerie Gillespie-de Laage, Paris
	Galerie Aronowitsch, Stockholm
1978	The Greenberg Gallery, St. Louis
	Galerie m, Bochum, West Germany
1979	Akron Art Institute, Akron, Ohio
	Paula Cooper Gallery, New York
	Galerie Gillespie-de Laage, Paris
	Ohio State University, Columbus
1980	The Whitechapel Art Gallery, London (travelled to Museum Haus Lange, Krefeld, West Germany, and Moderna Museet, Stockholm)
	Galerie Mukai, Tokyo
	Asher/Faure, Los Angeles
	Brooke Alexander Gallery, New York
	Delahunty Gallery, Dallas
	Paula Cooper Gallery, New York
	Bell Gallery, Brown University, Providence, Rhode Island (travelled to Georgia State University, Atlanta, and The Contemporary Arts Center, Cincinnati)
1981	Ackland Art Museum, University of North Carolina, Chapel Hill
	John Stoller Gallery, Minneapolis
	Daniel Weinberg Gallery, San Francisco
	The Israel Museum, Jerusalem
	Galerie Mukai, Tokyo
	Young-Hoffman Gallery, Chicago
1982	Paula Cooper Gallery, New York
	Portland Center for the Visual Arts, Portland, Oregon
	Susanne Hilberry Gallery, Birmingham, Michigan
	Yarlow/Salzman Gallery, Toronto
	Whitney Museum of American Art, New York (travelled to Dallas Museum of Fine Arts, Art Gallery of Ontario, Toronto, La Jolla Museum of Contemporary Art)
1983	Galerie Aronowitsch, Stockholm
	Paula Cooper Gallery, New York
	Asher/Faure, Los Angeles
1984	Paula Cooper Gallery, New York
	Galerie Aronowitsch, Stockholm
	Paula Cooper Gallery, New York
1985	Knoedler Kasmin, London
	Stedelijk Museum, Amsterdam (travelled to Kunstmuseum Dusseldorf and Staatliche Kunsthalle, Baden-Baden)
1986	Seattle Art Museum, Seattle, Washington
	Galerie Daniel Templon, Paris

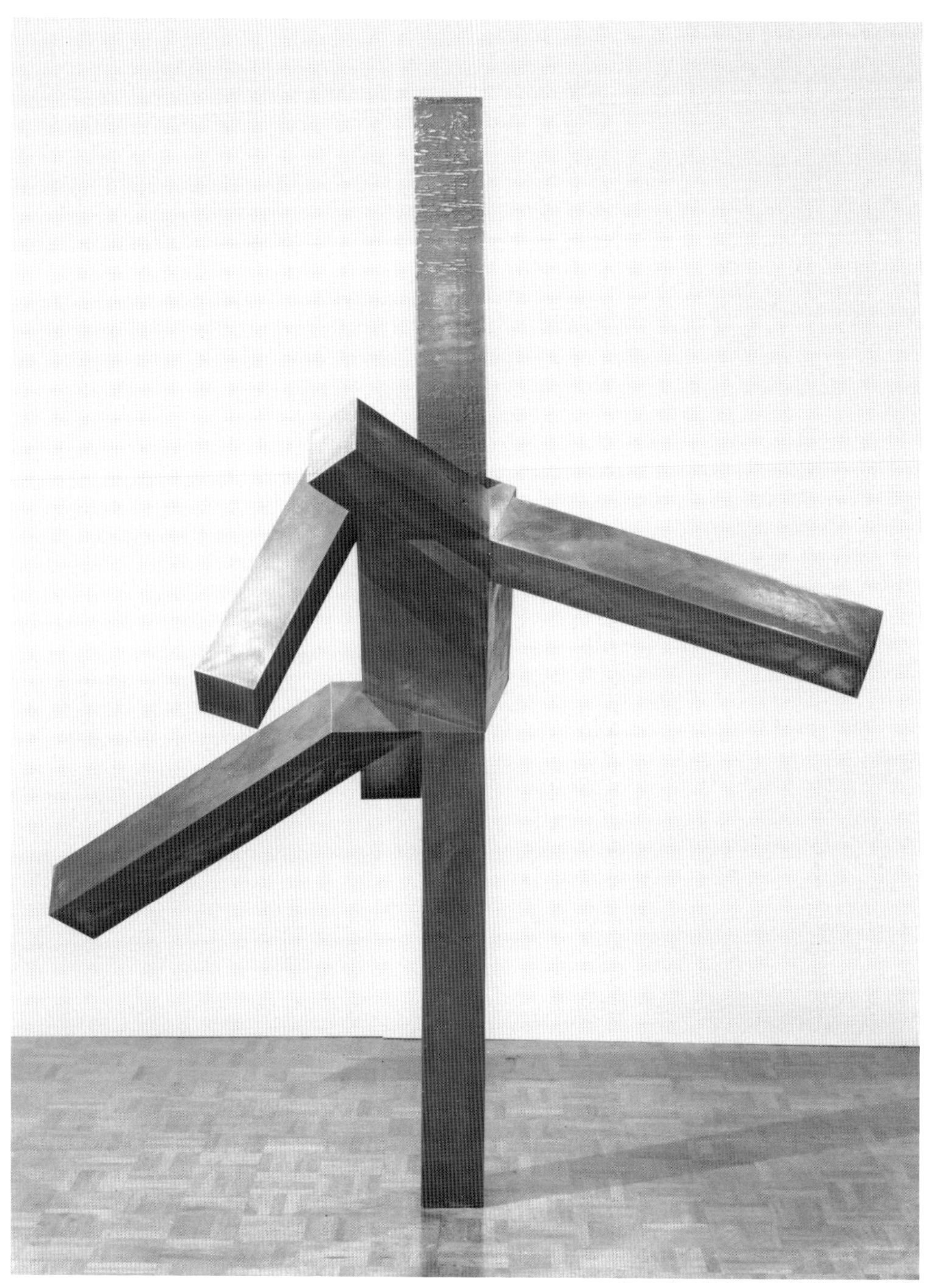

Fig. 26   Untitled, 1982
bronze A.P.
73 x 70 x 30″
Collection of the Artist

BIBLIOGRAPHY

Selected books, catalogues and periodical articles.

————, *Joel Shapiro*, Jerusalem, The Israel Museum, 1981.

Bloem, Marja and Karel Scampers, *Joel Shapiro*, Amsterdam:
The Stedelijk Museum, 1985.

Coplans, John, "Joel Shapiro: An Interview," *Dialogue*,
Akron Art Institute, January-February 1979, pp. 7-9.

Fields, Marc. "On Joel Shapiro's Sculpture and Drawings,"
Artforum 16, Summer, 1978, pp. 31-37.

Gettings, Frank, *Drawings 1974-1984*, Washington, D.C.:
The Hirshhorn Museum and Sculpture Garden, March 15-May 13,
1984, pp. 216-222.

Gilbert-Rolfe, Jeremy, "Joel Shapiro Works in Progress,"
Artforum, December 1973, pp. 73-74.

Hohl, Reinhold and Manfred Schneckenburger, *Documenta 6*,
Kassel: June-October 1977.

Jordy, William, *Joel Shapiro*, Providence, Rhode Island:
Brown University, Bell Gallery, 1981.

Kotik, Charlotta, "Joel Shapiro," *Figures: Forms and
Expressions*, Buffalo, New York: Albright-Knox Art Gallery,
CEPA Gallery, HALLWALLS, November 20, 1981 - January 3, 1982.

Krauss, Rosalind, *Joel Shapiro*, Chicago: The Museum of
Contemporary Art, September 11-November 7, 1976.

Krauss, Rosalind, *Passages in Modern Sculpture*, Cambridge,
Massachusetts: The M.I.T. Press, 1983.

Kuspit, Donald, "Manifest Densities," Art in America,
May 1983, pp. 148-152.

Marshall, Richard and Roberta Smith, *Joel Shapiro*, New York:
The Whitney Museum of American Art, October 21, 1982 -
January 2, 1983.

McShine, Kynaston, *An International Survey of Recent Painting
and Sculpture*, New York: The Museum of Modern Art, May 17 -
August 19, 1984.

Monte, James and Monica Tucker, *Anti-Illusion: Procedure/
Material*, New York: The Whitney Museum of American Art, 1969.

Ratcliff, Carter, "Joel Shapiro's Drawings," *The Print
Collector's Newsletter*, Vol. IX, #1, March-April 1978,
pp. 1-4.

SCULPTURE

Untitled, 1982 **(Fig. 26)**
bronze A.P.
73 x 70 x 30"
Collection of the Artist

Untitled, 1982-83 **(Fig. 10)**
cast bronze A.P.
43 x 34 x 35¾"
Collection of the Artist

Untitled, 1983 **(Fig. 8)**
Douglas Fir
86 x 18 x 49½"
Collection of the Artist

Untitled, 1982-83 **(Fig. 4)**
Bass wood
45½ x 38½ x 26½"
Collection of the Artist

Untitled, 1981-84 **(Fig. 11)**
bronze
47½ x 47 x 46½"
The Collection of Exxon Corporation

Untitled, 1983-84 **(Fig. 9)**
bronze 1/2
30 x 8½ x 11½"
The Newark Museum

Untitled, 1984 **(Fig. 2)**
cast iron
21½ x 29¼ x 5¾"
Courtesy Paula Cooper Gallery, New York

Untitled, 1984 **(Fig. 5)**
cast iron
5¼ x 24¼ x 41¾"
Collection of the Artist

Untitled, 1983-84 **(Fig. 12)**
bronze A.P.
80¾ x 52"
Collection of the Artist

Untitled, 1985
bronze 3/3
38½ x 28½ x 14"
The Detroit Institute of Arts
Gift of Martin Bernstein and Founders Society,
New Endowment Fund and General Endowment Fund

Untitled, 1985 **(Fig. 13)**
bronze 3/3
90¼ x 89¾ x 52½"
Courtesy Paula Cooper Gallery, New York

Untitled, 1985 **(Fig. 6)**
bronze A.P.
36¼ x 53 x 40"
Collection of the Artist

DRAWINGS

Untitled, 1981 **(Fig. 15)**
charcoal on paper
30⅛ x 36¼"
Sophie M. Friedman Fund
Courtesy, Museum of Fine Arts, Boston

Untitled, 1981 **(Fig. 16)**
charcoal on paper
26⅛ x 32⅜"
Gift of Laura Carpenter and Perry Bentley
Dallas Museum of Art

Untitled, 1982 **(Fig. 24)**
chalk and charcoal on paper
38 x 50"
The Museum of Contemporary Art, Los Angeles
The Barry Lowen Collection

Untitled, 1982-83 **(Fig. 22)**
charcoal and gouache on paper
40½ x 49⅞"
Mr. & Mrs. A. Skeppner

Untitled, 1985 **(Fig. 25)**
chalk and charcoal on paper
43 x 30¾"
General Mills Art Collection

Untitled, 1985 **(Fig. 14)**
chalk and charcoal on paper
43 x 30¾"
The Collection of Exxon Corporation

Untitled, 1985 **(Fig. 23)**
charcoal on paper
19 x 26"
Mr. & Mrs. Gilbert Edelson

Untitled, 1985 **(Fig. 17)**
charcoal and gouache on paper
43¼ x 30⅞"
Paula Cooper Gallery, New York

Untitled, 1985 **(Fig. 21)**
charcoal on paper
43¼ x 30¾"
Private Collection, Boston

Untitled, 1985 **(Fig. 18)**
charcoal on paper
43 x 30¾"
Collection of Mr. & Mrs. Robert Quinn

Untitled, 1985 **(Fig. 19)**
charcoal on paper
44 x 30¾"
Keny and Johnson Gallery

Untitled, 1985 **(Fig. 20)**
charcoal on paper
43 x 30¾"
Collection of Mr. & Mrs. Robert Buford

RINGLING MUSEUM STAFF

Office of the Director

Laurence J. Ruggiero
Director

Myriam A. Springuel
Assistant to the Director, Curatorial

Kathleen G. Chilson
Executive Secretary

Public Affairs

Robert L. Ardren
Public Affairs Director

Curatorial

Cynthia Duval
Decorative Arts

Anthony F. Janson
European Art

Joseph Jacobs
20th Century Art

Mark Ormond
Exhibitions

Education

Nancy J. Glaser
Head of Education/Museum Liaison Officer

Marianna M. Adams
Community and School Programs

Susan M. Burkhart
Docent and Visitor Services

Conservation

Michelle A. Scalera
Museum Conservator

Library

Lynell A. Morr
Librarian

Administrative Services

Gerald C. Boon
Chief Financial Officer

Edwin M. Morrison
Chief of Operations

Elizabeth S. Telford
Head of Support Services

Pamela A. Palmer
Registrar

William J. McDaniels
Buildings Superintendent

John W. Janowski
Head of Grounds

Ronald E. Peterson
Chief of Security

Museum Foundation

H. Douglas Kerr
Executive Director

Membership

Abigail L. Whitenack
Membership manager